www.wadsworth.com

www.wadsworth.com is the World Wide Web site for Thomson Wadsworth and is your direct source to dozens of online resources.

At *www.wadsworth.com* you can find out about supplements, demonstration software, and student resources. You can also send email to many of our authors and preview new publications and exciting new technologies.

www.wadsworth.com
Changing the way the world learns®

On Ethics
and Living Well

On Ethics
and Living Well

ROBERT C. SOLOMON
University of Texas, Austin

THOMSON
—————✳————— ™
WADSWORTH

Australia · Canada · Mexico · Singapore · Spain
United Kingdom · United States

THOMSON
＊
™
WADSWORTH

Publisher/Executive Editor: *Holly J. Allen*
Acquisitions Editor: *Steve Wainwright*
Assistant Editor: *Lee McCracken and Anna Lustig*
Editorial Assistant: *Barbara Hillaker*
Technology Project Manager: *Julie Aguilar*
Marketing Manager: *Worth Hawes*
Marketing Assistant: *Andrew Keay*
Marketing Communications Manager: *Bryan Vann, Vicky Wan, and Laurel Anderson*

Project Manager, Editorial Production: *Brenda Ginty*
Art Director: *Maria Epes*
Print Buyer: *Lisa Claudeanos*
Permissions Editor: *Chelsea Junget*
Production Service: *M.R. Carey, Cadmus*
Copy Editor: *Jill Amack*
Indexer: *Erin Frank*
Cover Designer: *Bruce Saltzman*
Compositor: *Cadmus*
Cover and Text Printer: *Thomson West*

Printed in the United States of America
1 2 3 4 5 6 7 09 08 07 06 05

For more information about our products, contact us at:
Thomson Learning Academic Resource Center
1-800-423-0563

For permission to use material from this text or product, submit a request online at **http://www.thomsonrights.com**. Any additional questions about permissions can be submitted by email to **thomsonrights@thomson.com**.

Library of Congress Control Number: 2004115480

ISBN 0-495-00295-X

Thomson Higher Education
10 Davis Drive
Belmont, CA 94002-3098
USA

Asia (including India)
Thomson Learning
5 Shenton Way
#01-01 UIC Building
Singapore 068808

Australia/New Zealand
Thomson Learning Australia
102 Dodds Street
Southbank, Victoria 3006
Australia

Canada
Thomson Nelson
1120 Birchmount Road
Toronto, Ontario M1K 5G4
Canada

UK/Europe/Middle East/Africa
Thomson Learning
High Holborn House
50–51 Bedford Road
London WC1R 4LR
United Kingdom

Latin America
Thomson Learning
Seneca, 53
Colonia Polanco
11560 Mexico
D.F. Mexico

Spain (including Portugal)
Thomson Paraninfo
Calle Magallanes, 25
28015 Madrid, Spain

For Jem, Jesi, Dani, Rachel, Carrie, and, of course, for Kathy

Contents

Preface

I n this book I have tried to provide a very short and straightforward, but reasonably comprehensive, introduction to ethics. Questions about "values" and "contemporary American morality" have always been much in the news, but today the demand for education in ethics is especially loud and clear. What is not always so clear, however, is what is to be taught under this title. In fact, ethics is one of those subjects that is so imperative and so controversial that even its definition is a matter of considerable dispute. Does ethics require an absolute set of rules that apply to everyone, everywhere, and at all times? If so, do these rules come from God and religion or from the laws and customs of society? Is there room for legitimate disagreement about even the most basic ethical principles? To what extent is morality personal and individual, and to what extent does it depend on the nature of the particular situation? Should ethics focus on obeying rules or personal character, or are these ultimately the same? Is being moral just "doing the right thing" or does it require right thinking and feeling as well? And what is morality? Is it first of all obeying the rules or is it primarily a concern for the well-being of other people? Is there a difference between morality and ethics? Is it behavior alone that counts or should we also be concerned with the intentions and motives from which action springs?

In what follows I develop a brief and basic introduction to the various views and theories that have ruled much of philosophical, as well as popular, thinking for the past two and a half thousand years or so. While I have included brief accounts of some of the theories of the most influential philosophers, I have emphasized the patterns of controversy and concern rather than the details of those theories or the facts about the philosophers themselves. (A very brief set of biographies can be found in the appendix to Chapter 1.) I have tried to be fair in my presentation, but in my effort to keep this book readable and easily digestible for beginning students I have inevitably oversimplified the considerable subtlety of a great many ongoing disputes in favor of more memorable summaries and outlines. I have not attempted to avoid controversy—which is, after all, the very heart of the subject—but I have attempted to be as neutral as possible in the presentation of the various ethical viewpoints and theories. For example, I have allowed myself to express some reservations about a good deal of modern moral philosophy in a short account of Nietzsche's attack on morality, and I have taken more seriously than usual the often under-fire thesis called "relativism," the claim that what is morally right in one society may not be morally right in another. In a global age of competing absolutes it seems to me that some balance between absolutism and a plurality of religions, cultures, and values is not only timely, but obligatory.

While Chapters 1 and 2 cover fairly conventional concepts and theories of ethics, Chapter 3 provides more than the usual space for the rather new (but in fact very old) philosophy of "virtue ethics." Virtue ethics is an ethical viewpoint that emphasizes personal character rather than abstract moral principles or the consequences of our actions. I believe that these various approaches to ethics are complementary rather than contradictory, but I would argue that the traditional overemphasis on rules and results has seriously misrepresented the nature of our ordinary moral judgments. The omission of an adequate appreciation of the virtues and the neglect of a general account of the good life have too often threatened to render moral philosophy irrelevant to the everyday concerns about values and ethics that have received so much attention lately. In deliberating our own actions and in judging others, we do in fact pay a great deal of attention to "what kind of a person" one is or wants to be. I have therefore given virtue ethics a prominent place in my account here.

The issues of ethics are the issues of life and living in human society. We do not just behave according to instinct or impulse, and we do not live alone. We think and deliberate. We have goals and ideals. We willingly conform to patterns of acceptable social behavior and we share in praise for certain sorts of actions (generosity and bravery, for example) and condemn others (utter selfishness and cowardice, for instance). We obey the law, but may well disagree with some particular law on the basis of some "higher" principle. We accept these principles in turn for further reasons that we may agree or disagree about. And however personal and individual we consider our values to be, we share certain very general aspirations, for example, the need for self-respect, the means to living a decent life, the importance of love and friendship in our lives, and the importance of doing the right thing—although we may not always agree on just what that is. It would be a mistake, however, to think of the variety of theories and concerns in ethics as a "grab bag" or smorgasbord from which everyone can pick and choose according to personal taste. Indeed, if there is one overview that has motivated philosophers since Plato, it is the idea that there is a *correct* theory of ethics, that the goals, ideals, virtues, rules, and principles governing behavior do form a more or less coherent and comprehensible system, which it is the purpose of the study of ethics to understand.

On the other hand, however, it is an obvious truth that people often have conflicts of interest and disagreements about what is the right thing to do, what is the ideal way to be, and what is the best way to live. The history of ethics shows us how philosophers disagree. Nevertheless, the reason why we disagree both in particular cases and in the most general philosophical debates, is that each of us believes that we are *right*. Tolerance (and "relativism") have their limits. Ethics, unlike one's favorite flavor of ice cream, is not just a matter of taste. Our actions and our moral judgments can be challenged, and we are expected to have reasons to back them up. When we disagree in ethics, our differences of opinion can become bitter, even violent. Accordingly, it is necessary to understand the views we disagree about and come to grips with the nature of those disagreements. But understanding the other side does not mean giving up one's own convictions. Appreciating the variety of ethical theories does not mean "it's all a matter of opinion" but neither does it mean that everyone else is wrong.

The aim of the study of ethics and the aim of this book is to help students think about ethical issues, from the most concrete personal problems ("I promised my high school sweetheart that I wouldn't go out with anyone else while I'm away at college, but then I met. . .") and more abstract puzzles and paradoxes ("Why would a person act against his or her own best interests?" and "What's wrong with blackmail, if it's an exercise of freedom of speech?") to the most general ethical questions ("What is happiness?" and "How do you resolve a conflict of fundamental principles?"). Ethical theories have been formulated to help us think about right conduct in the concrete situations of life, to organize the enormous number of opinions, feelings, and "intuitions" we have about what is right and what is wrong. At the same time, particular personal problems often arise just because of our awareness of the broader ethical questions. What seems like an innocent action may nevertheless set a disturbing precedent. A course of action might further one's personal ambitions, but only by breaking some basic moral rule (for example, the prohibition against lying) or by violating one's personal sense of integrity.

Our awareness of the consequences and the significance of our actions adds a dimension to our thinking. A student knows that he or she will have a better chance of getting a job with a small fabrication on the résumé; but even if no one will ever find out, what does it mean to have lied? A person wants "out" of a tedious marriage because his or her happiness seems to lie elsewhere. But what does it mean to abandon a marriage, to back out of one's marriage vows, and how will this affect everyone else involved? Ethics involves the unity of concrete human concerns and a more general awareness and appreciation of worthy goals, ideals, virtues, rules, and principles. If we may play off a phrase from one of the great moral philosophers, Immanuel Kant, we might say that ethics without reference to particular actions and feelings is empty, but action and feelings devoid of ethics are blind.

One of the underlying messages in this book is that ethics is a shared effort. My debts to friends, teachers, colleagues, and students are in evidence on every one of the following pages. (I refrain from blaming them for any mistakes.) Insofar as this book has a bias, it is toward virtue ethics and a bit of existentialism. Nevertheless I have tried to be fair toward the classical ethical theories. Those theories I digested under the tutelage of Betty Flowers, Charles Stevenson, William Frankena, Julius Moravsik, and Stuart Hampshire. The rise of virtue ethics I trace back to Aristotle and more recently, Nietzsche, but I give special credit to Alasdair MacIntyre, William Gass, Frithjof Bergmann, Edmund Pincoffs, Bernard Williams, Martha Nussbaum,

Christine Swanton, and others for making it so prominent today. I owe several old but special debts of gratitude to Lee Bowie and Meredith Michaels, Paul Woodruff, Kathleen Higgins, Shirley Hull, Elaine Engelhardt, and Janet McCracken. Several friends and colleagues in the publishing world helped give birth to the book, beginning with Kaye Pace of McGraw-Hill, who first helped me develop and publish the book, and David Tatom, who brought it to Harcourt. My thanks to Steve Wainwright and Bob Talisse of Wadsworth for supporting the present edition. My thanks also to the dozen or so readers who have reviewed and criticized the various drafts of the book and to the many students who have been my audience for so many years. Here, for another new generation, is the latest version.

Robert C. Solomon
Austin, Texas

1

Introduction to Ethics

L ast Thursday, you went out for lunch with an acquaintance from class, a nice enough fellow, but not a candidate for lifelong friendship. As you were wolfing down your last bite of cheeseburger, you suddenly flushed: you realized that you had forgotten your wallet. You were flat broke. Embarrassed, you entreated your classmate to lend you five dollars, which you would, of course, pay back on Tuesday. Today is Wednesday; you forgot.

Now you are doubly embarrassed, for having had to borrow the money in the first place, then for having forgotten to pay it back when promised. You are tempted, momentarily, to ignore the entire awkward situation, just to assume—what may well be true—that your classmate has forgotten about the loan (after all, it is only five dollars). But maybe he hasn't forgotten, or, at least, he will no doubt remember it when he sees you. For an irrational instant, you consider dropping the course and disappearing from view, but then you realize that would be ridiculous, the five dollars just isn't that important. It is highly unlikely—it would be rather embarrassing for him—that he would actually confront you and ask you for the money.

Nor would he very likely make a big deal out of it and talk to other people about your unethical behavior. Anyway, you aren't close friends and don't generally talk to each other. So what's the difference?

But now, small hints of large doubts start interrupting your day. You've made up your mind. You will just ignore the debt and ignore him. You are convinced that no harm or further embarrassment will come to you. The fellow probably knows none of your friends and it is hardly likely that he will announce to the class or put a personal ad in the paper that you are a deadbeat. And yet, it's ruining your day, and it may well ruin other days. "If only I could get rid of this guilty feeling," you say to yourself. But it is not just a feeling; it is a new and wholly unwelcome sense of who you are. A soft voice inside of you (sometimes it sounds like your own voice; occasionally it seems to be your mother's) keeps whispering, "Deadbeat . . . deadbeat" (and worse).

Already distracted from your work, you start speculating, "What if we all were to forget about our debts?" Your first response is that you would probably be washing dishes at the Burger Shoppe, since no one would ever lend anyone money and your classmate would never have lent money to you. Your second response to yourself is that "Not everyone forgets," but this argument doesn't make you feel any better. It reminds you that in a world where most people pay their debts, you are one of the scoundrels who does not. You start rationalizing: "After all," you say to yourself, "I need the money more than he does." In a final moment of belligerence, you smash your fist on the table in the library and say, in part to yourself and in part to the slightly surprised people sharing your table, "The only person I have to worry about is me!"

There is an embarrassed silence. Then you walk over to the bank of phones and dial: "Hello, Harris? You remember that five dollars you loaned me? . . ."

■ ■ ■

The point of this little scenario is to capture the day-to-day nature of ethics. Even such a simple situation involves conflicting interests, profound moral principles, questions of character, and the nagging voice of conscience, culminating in a quiet, but nevertheless telling, conclusion concerning the sort of person you are. This case does not involve any of the more notoriously difficult social problems and life-or-death decisions so vehemently debated today such as the abortion issue, the legitimacy of "preemptive" war, the plight of the homeless in a land of affluence, or starving children in a world awash with surplus food. But, ultimately, the considerations that enter into our debates on these global issues reflect our habits and opinions and our ways of thinking about the most ordinary circumstances. Our politics express who we are and what we believe, and even our most abstract ideologies reveal (although often in a convoluted and even reactionary way) the principles and prejudices of everyday life.

WHAT IS ETHICS?

Ethics is that part of philosophy which is concerned with living well, being a good person, doing the right thing, getting along with other people, and wanting the right things in life. Ethics is essential to living in society, any society, with its various traditions, practices, and institutions. Of course, those traditions, practices, and institutions can and must themselves be assessed according to ethical standards, but they themselves determine many of the rules and expectations that define the ethical outlook of the people living within them. Ethics therefore has both a social and a personal dimension, but it is not at all easy, in theory or in practice, to separate these. Moral judgment is both the product of society and one of its constitutive features. What we call our "personal values" are for the most part learned together and shared by a great many people. Indeed, those values we consider most personal are typically not those that are most idiosyncratic, but rather those that are most common and most profound: respect for human (and animal) life, outrage at being the victim of a lie, compassion for those much worse off than yourself, and an insistence on personal integrity in the face of adversity.

The word "ethics" refers both to a discipline—the study of our values and their justification—and to the subject matter of that discipline—the actual values and rules of the conduct by which we live. The two meanings merge in the fact that we behave (and misbehave) according to a complex and continually changing set of rules, customs, and expectations; consequently, we are forced to reflect on our conduct and attitudes, to justify and sometimes to revise them.

Why do we need to study ethics as a discipline? Isn't it enough that we *have* ethics, that we do (most of us, most of the time) act according to our values and rules? But part of our ethics is understanding ethics, that is, acting for *reasons* and being able to defend our actions if called upon to do so. It is not enough, after the age of eight or so, simply to do what you are told; it is just as important to know the reason why, and to be able to say no when you think an act is wrong. So, too, it is not enough to have strong political opinions on this or that controversial social issue. It is important to have reasons, to have a larger vision, to have a framework within which to house and defend your opinions. The study of ethics teaches us to appreciate the overall system of reasons within which having ethics makes sense. Understanding what we are doing and why is just as essential to ethics as the doing itself.

We learn ethics, typically, a lesson at a time. Our education begins in childhood, first and foremost, with continuous demonstrations of "normal" behavior. We watch our parents and our older siblings before we know what they are doing, and we imitate them, no doubt before we know what we are doing. Our education continues with a number of instructions and prohibitions, such as "Don't hit your little sister" and "You should share your toys with your friends." The recognition of authority is essential, of course, beginning with "You do what your father says" and culminating in "Because it's the law, that's why." But it is also learning reasons, such as "Because if everyone did that, there wouldn't be any left" or "Because it will make her unhappy." Eventually, we learn the specialized language of *morality* and its more abstract reasons for doing or refraining from certain actions, such as "Because it is your duty" and "Because it is immoral." By this time we have begun to learn that ethics is not just a varied collection of "dos and don'ts," but a *system* of values and principles that tie together in a reasonable and coherent way in order to make our society and our lives as "civilized" and as happy as possible. The study of ethics is the final step in this process of education—the understanding of that system as such and the way that all our particular values and principles fit into it.

CHANGE, CHOICE, AND "PLURALISM"

Our understanding of ethics is complicated enormously by the fact that, as a living system, our ethics is continually *changing*. Consider, for example, the tremendous changes that our society has experienced over just the past few decades in the realm of sexual morality; today we accept behavior that would have been wanton immorality fifty years ago (for example, topless beachwear for *men!*). Similar changes have taken place in our concept of personal roles and career options. Only twenty years ago, many people considered it "unethical" for a wife to work except in cases of dire family need, but it was perfectly acceptable—in fact, even commendable—for a husband to spend so much time working at his career that he virtually never saw his children or did anything but work. Today, we do not find such behavior praiseworthy but, rather, akin to a disease—some call it workaholism. And women, of course, work just as hard at their careers as men. Attitudes toward authority have also changed dramatically. Fifty years ago, the attitude of most young men when drafted into the army (or invited to enlist) was unquestioning acceptance. Twenty-five years ago, those who refused to follow orders and resisted authority were praised by many people as moral heroes. What this means and whether there are more basic values that support both obedience and disobedience (depending on the situation) are some of the most important questions of ethics.

We live in a society filled with change and disagreement, in which each generation is taught to reexamine the values and actions of the older generation; doing what you are told or simply conforming to tradition is not necessarily a mark of moral goodness, but may be considered cowardice or lack of character. Our ethics, in other words, essentially involves *choice*. In fact, having and permitting individual freedom of choice is itself one of the most noteworthy values of our ethics. But choice is not arbitrary, and to choose between alternative courses of action or opposed values requires intelligent deliberation and some sense of the reasons why we should choose one rather than another. Each of us must select a way of life, perhaps a career or a profession, perhaps a long search for selfhood or a life of creativity or adventure. We might "follow in our parents' footsteps" or we might go off on a completely different path. But we must choose. Each of us must decide whether or not to get married, and when and to whom. We must decide whether or not to have children, how many, and how they will be raised, thus affecting the lives of others in the most direct and dramatic sense possible. Every day, each of us decides whether or not to engage in a dozen small misdeeds and an occasional misdemeanor, such as whether to drive high-speed Highway 10 to El Paso at a safe (but illegal) 80 miles per hour, or to take an extra box of paperclips from the office, since "no one will ever miss them."

The importance of choice in ethics is often confused with the notion that we "choose our values," that values are merely "subjective," that everyone has his or her own "personal values." This is misleading. Most of ethics involves decisions between already-established possibilities and already-available reasons, and those we do not choose. A student deciding between joining the navy or going to law school does indeed have an important choice to make, but the alternatives and their values are provided by the society as a whole. (There must already be a navy to join or a society with a role for lawyers.) One does not choose the alternatives; one chooses from among the alternatives. And once one has chosen, he or she is suddenly situated in a world of "objective" values—the ironclad rules of the military or the ethics of the legal profession. In ethics we face choices, but the personal values we thereby endorse are virtually never one's own values alone. The very nature of values is such that they must be shared; they exist over and above those who embrace them.

Nevertheless, there is a sense, defended recently by the French existentialist Jean-Paul Sartre, in which each of us "chooses" our values every time we make an ethical decision. By deciding not to take advantage of a loophole in the tax laws, for example, one personally affirms the priority of compliance over individual gain. By acting in one way rather than another, we support one value rather than another, one sense of who we are rather than another. Thus, Sartre also says that we "choose ourselves," that ethics is largely a matter of individual choice and commitment rather than of obedience to already-established authorities.

We live in an ethically *pluralist* society. This means that there is no single code of ethics but several different sets of values and rules in a variety of contexts, communities, and subcultures. Professionals and businesspeople in our society emphasize individual success and mobility; some cultural communities stress the importance of group identity and stable ethnic tradition. Some college and urban communities are notably more liberal in their tolerance for eccentricity and deviance than the more conservative suburban neighborhoods surrounding them. Even what would seem to be the most basic rules of morality seem to vary from culture to culture, context to context, and neighborhood to neighborhood. Thus, we find our Supreme Court—the ultimate arbiter of laws, if not morals—insisting on community standards as the test for what is permissible, in the case of pornography, for instance. Such disagreements cut to the very core of our ethical values. Many people in our society insist that the ultimate value is individual freedom. But freedom has its costs, among them the inconvenience and deprivation of others, and many people thus argue there are issues of morality and justice that are more important than individual freedom. Some people consider it absolutely wrong to take a human life, even if the life in question is that of an unborn zygote or fetus; others do not believe that such a life counts as "human" and should be sacrificed if necessary to the well-being of the mother. None of these differences in ethics are easily reconciled; in fact, they may be irreconcilable. But that makes it all the more important that we understand the nature of these differences, and at least know how to try to reconcile our differences instead of intransigently shouting our views at one another, using the law to legislate morality, or simply storming out of the room. Trying to be reasonable in this sense is much of what ethical discussion and debate are about, and pluralism provides much of the motive. If we aren't clear about the nature and justification of our own values, we won't be in a position to understand the nature and justification of other people's values. And if we don't understand other people's values, neither will we understand how they conflict or might be brought into harmony with our own.

ETHICS AND ETHOS

The word "ethics" comes from the Greek word *ethos,* meaning "character" or "custom," and the derivative phrase *ta ethika,* which the philosophers Plato and Aristotle used to describe their own studies of Greek values and ideals. Accordingly, ethics is first of all a concern for individual character, including what we blandly call "being a good person," but it is also a concern for the overall character of an entire society, which is still appropriately called its "ethos." Ethics is participation in and an understanding of an ethos, the effort to understand the social rules which govern and limit our behavior, especially those fundamental rules, such as the prohibitions on killing and stealing and the commandments that one should "honor thy parents" and respect the rights of others, which we call *morality.*

The close connection between ethics and social customs ("mores," which shares its etymological root with the word "morality") inevitably raises the question of whether morality is *nothing but* the customs of our particular society, our ethics nothing but the rules of our particular ethos. On the one hand, it is clear that ethics and morality are very closely tied to the laws and the customs of a particular society. Kissing in public and making an enormous profit in a business transaction are considered immoral in some societies, not in others. But, on the other hand, we are firmly convinced that not *all* laws or customs endorsed by an entire society are equally acceptable. The rules of etiquette may be merely a matter of local custom or taste, but the prohibition against cannibalism, for example, seems to have much more universal power and justification than the simple reminder, "That just isn't done around here."

One way of circumscribing the principles of morality—as distinguished from rules of etiquette and standards of good taste, for example—is to insist that these are not the province of only a particular society or subculture within a society, but rather rules that we apply to all people everywhere and expect them to obey. We might be happy to accept, and even be charmed by, the fact that people in another culture eat food with wooden sticks instead of forks or enjoy music based on quarter tones without a discernible melody. But when we consider the "culture" of gangland America, for example, or the peculiar rules of certain cults and subcultures, our tolerance diminishes and we find ourselves quite willing to "impose" our values and standards. Ethics provides the basic rules of an ethos, but those rules are not limited to that ethos. Ethics needs a culture in which to be cultivated, but that does not mean that ethics consists of just the rules of that particular culture. Morality, according to many philosophers, is that set of rules which applies to *all* cultures, whatever their customs or traditions.

An ethos is that core of attitudes, beliefs, and feelings that gives coherence and vitality to a people (in ancient Greek, an *ethnos,* a word significantly similar to "ethos"). It may be spelled out explicitly in terms of laws, but much of an ethos resides in the hearts and minds of the people, in what they expect of one another and what they expect of themselves, in what they like and dislike, in what they value and disdain, hope and fear. It is an essential part of our ethos, for example, that individual success and "standing out in the crowd" are very important to us. There is no law or moral principle that commands that this should be so, but obviously our ethics very much depends upon these values of individualism and achievement. In some societies, by way of contrast, individual ambitions and eccentricities are unacceptable. "The nail that sticks out is the one that gets hammered down," reads a traditional Japanese proverb. We should not assume that all *ethè* (the plural of ethos) are the same, even in their most basic values and visions.

MORALITY

Ethics includes the whole range of acceptable social and personal practices, from the rules of common courtesy to the institutions that determine the kinds of work we do, the kinds of friends we have, and the ways we relate to both family and strangers. Morality, on the other hand, is something more specific, a subset of ethical rules which are of particular importance and transcend the boundaries of any particular ethos or situation. Thus, we believe, it is *always* immoral to be cruel to children, even if doing so is part of a family tradition for several generations. "Morality," accordingly, is thought to be a weightier term than ethics. If someone refuses to play fair or to honor a verbal contract, we might say that he or she is untrustworthy or unethical, but we would not say immoral. If a person abuses children or poisons his in-laws, however, we would call such behavior immoral, thus indicating the seriousness of these violations. Morality consists of the most basic and inviolable rules of a society.

The distinction between ethics and morality—ethics as the whole of our sense of self and our place in society and morality as the core, universal, most inviolable rules in any society—is not always followed in either ordinary conversation or philosophical theorizing. Indeed, the curious history of these terms shows how much our very conception of ethics and morality has shifted over the centuries, along with the more obvious shifts in the practices they evaluate and prescribe. The current definition of the word "morality," for example, displays a range of meanings that shows both the ancient sense in which the terms morality and ethics both embrace the whole of human behavior and the very narrow nineteenth-century concern in which sexual behavior became an obsessive focus of ethical concern. The *Random House Dictionary,* for example, lists as definitions of morality: "(a) conformity to rules of right conduct, (b) moral quality of character, (c) virtue in sexual matters, (d) a doctrine or system of morals, and (e) moral instruction." We shall see how these various conceptions play off against one another in current as well as traditional debates in ethics. But for our purposes here, we shall start by sticking fairly closely to the first definition of morality as "conformity to rules of right conduct"—and as those rules themselves. But this is not sufficient. Many rules in ethics ("don't be rude") and even in etiquette ("don't eat your burrito with a spoon") seem to be rules of right conduct. What distinguishes *moral* rules is a number of rather distinctive features, which are emphasized (in different ways and with

9

many mixed opinions) by philosophers and other moral theorists. Here are four of the most-often mentioned:

1. Moral Rules Have Great *Importance*. Moral rules, however else they may be characterized, are of indisputable importance. They are like trump cards in certain games, overpowering all other considerations. In our opening example, the *obligation* to repay a loan outweighs purely personal concerns, such as one's embarrassment or one's own need for money. Indeed, it is the mark of morality that the amount of money involved is not what is important. The obligation would override self-interest whether the amount involved were ten cents or a thousand dollars. It is sometimes suggested that moral rules are those without which a society could not survive, or at least could not function in what it considers a civilized way. For example, how could there be promises or contracts at all—the basis of much of our lives—if the respect for promises and contracts were not more important than a person's personal advantage in breaking them? Furthermore, to call a person or an act "immoral" is to condemn that person or act in the strongest possible terms, just as to say that an issue is a moral issue is to say that it is of the utmost urgency.

One problem with characterizing moral issues in terms of their extreme importance, however, is that this reduces the insistence that any particular moral issue is important to a mere tautology, the trivial demand that it is important because it is important. Some matters concerning a person's private sexual behavior, for instance, are considered moral issues but, in the larger scheme of things, hardly seem very important. And some of the most global issues confronting us, international politics and wars which threaten the lives of millions, while indisputably important, are often not treated by State Department officials as moral questions at all. Therefore, while it is generally true that moral issues are important issues and that one way of emphasizing the importance of an issue is to designate it a moral issue, importance alone does not seem to be adequate to capture what we ordinarily mean by morality. There can be petty moral issues, and there can be extremely important nonmoral issues.

2. Morality Consists of *Universal Rules*. Morality is rule-governed in that it tells us what sorts of things to do and not to do, by way of general classes and types of acts, such as "one ought to repay debts" and "don't ever tell a lie." Morality involves obedience of such rules, but it also requires understanding and knowledge of the rules, and the recognition that they are necessary and obligatory. Furthermore, moral rules are distinguished by the fact that they are *universal:* they apply to everyone, everywhere. They are not just local customs or the rules of some particular practice (such as staying behind the line of scrimmage in football).

One problem with characterizing morality in terms of obedience to rules is that it seems to leave out a great deal of behavior that is, in an important sense, mindless. Good habits are as important in ethics as they are in etiquette and sports, and the very nature of a habit is such that its actions are nondeliberative, unthinking. Of course, habitual behavior can *conform* to a moral principle, but this weakens the notion of obedience considerably. And is it true that all of what we consider moral can be captured in a genuine principle? The demand that we should "love our neighbors" has the form of a principle, but does it capture the spirit of love that one should express affection *on principle?* Can the notion of rules capture all of the aspects of morality, for instance, the role of the right feelings in moral behavior? Or is obedience of certain rules just one aspect of morality and not morality as such?

The question of universality, of course, is one of the central controversies in ethics. Again, moral principles may be universal in form ("everyone ought to . . .") but the scope of the "everyone" remains in question. Does it mean everyone in the world, or everyone in this society, or everyone "like us," or, the most trivial, everyone who is in the same relevant circumstances? At the minimum, moral principles can't be designated for one and only one person. "John Jones ought to . . ." is not and cannot be a moral principle (even if, indeed, John Jones ought to).

3. Moral Rules Are *Rational, Disinterested,* and *Objective.* There are special *reasons* for acting morally, for example, "because it is my obligation." These reasons require special concepts (e.g., duty, obligation, on principle) and a special kind of upbringing in which these concepts are inculcated. This ability to think in terms of abstract principles (e.g., "never tell a lie") and reasons (e.g., "because if everyone lied, no one could believe anyone") is often called *rationality.* One of the key features of rationality, according to many philosophers, is its universality. Unlike most emotions and desires, for example, reason is the same in everyone. Everyone may have his or her own ideal of love or pet peeve, but we all necessarily share the conclusions of reason, e.g. "two plus two equals four." Thus it is sometimes said that, if a reason is a good reason, it will be so "for every rational creature," and morality has

11

been defined by some philosophers as the rules and actions of "a completely rational person." The hard question then, of course, is whether rationality is itself objective and universal, or whether what counts as "practical reason" in ethics might differ from culture to culture. (It also differs from philosophical theory to philosophical theory.)

It is also said that morality is rational, in part, because it is *disinterested*. A moral rule is disinterested both in that it applies without regard to one's own personal interests or feelings or status in the case and in that it remains oblivious to the interests, feelings, and status of the people to whom it applies. (Think of the classic image of Justice wearing a blindfold, and thus being "blind" to individual interests and the identities of the people who stand before her.) One has an obligation to repay a loan whether or not one needs the money, whether or not repaying the loan will advance one's interests in other ways (for example, making it easier to obtain another loan in the future), and whether or not the person who made the loan needs the money back. Of course, one can sometimes use a moral principle to one's own advantage, but the moral principle itself is formulated to no one's advantage and with no particular person's interests in mind. To so insist that morality is independent of subjective feelings and interests is to say that morality is *objective*. Thus rationality and disinterestedness imply objectivity. "Adultery is wrong!" does not mean "I don't like adultery" or "Our society disapproves of adultery"; a moral rule is objective insofar as its correctness is quite distinct from what particular people—or even whole societies—happen to think of it. "What's right is right and what's wrong is wrong." (*Subjectivity,* by contrast, is often dismissed as the notion that morals are only "one's own personal opinion" and nothing more.)

Again, however, the scope of this feature of morality can be called into question. Is rationality (that is, thoughtfulness and deliberation) essential to all moral behavior, or is unthinking, habitual performance sometimes far more impressive? Should morality be disinterested? Perhaps in the case of justice or an actual judge in a courtroom, but should we praise parents for disinterestedly raising their children, or friends for disinterestedly doing what they ought to do, for example, visiting a sick friend in the hospital? So, too, with objectivity. If objectivity rather than subjectivity means little more than a defensible, not merely personal opinion, then there may be no objection to it (though even then, with reference to such personal feelings as love and grief, there are hard questions to be raised). But if objectivity is taken to mean that there are moral facts in the world, quite independent of our feelings, interests, and attitudes, then the notion of objectivity becomes quite controversial.

4. Morality Is *Concerned with Other People*. Morality essentially involves consideration of interests other than one's own and is thus well summarized in the various versions of the so-called Golden Rule. "Do unto others as you would have them do unto you" is found in almost every ethical system. In the Hebrew Talmud, for example, it is presented as the basic principle of ethics: "What is hurtful to yourself do not to your fellow man; that is the whole of the Torah [the Jewish Scriptures] and the remainder is but commentary." The Confucian *Analects* tell us, "Do not unto others what you would not they should do unto you." The Taoist *T'ai Shang Kan Ying Pien* says, "Regard your neighbor's gain as your own gain, and regard your neighbor's loss as your own loss." The Buddha insisted, "Hurt not others with that which pains yourself," and Mohammed commanded (as in the *Analects*), "Do not unto others what you would not they should do unto you." The slight differences among these versions of the rule may make a considerable difference in morals. Consider the difference, for example, between the warning that what you do to others might be done to you in turn, and the appeal to compassion, that you should think about other people's feelings in the same way that you think of your own. It is worth noting that most of the versions refer to one's own possible pains and interests. But at the same time, every version makes reference to the interests of other people, and this is the essence of morality; it presupposes an awareness of the interests of others as well as of one's own. (We might note that even the cynical version, "Do unto others before they do unto you," presupposes awareness of other people's interests and intentions but construes these in a strictly antagonistic way.) The opposition between morality and mere self-interest, however, does not imply that to be moral you must always go against your own self-interest. Indeed, one of the most common arguments for morality is that it ultimately serves all of our self-interest and, all things considered, it is to our advantage that everyone (including us) obeys the rules of morality and pays attention to the interests and well-being of others.

Again, however, the criterion comes into question when we begin asking what makes an action moral rather than, say, kind or considerate. To care for other people is undoubtedly a good thing, but one can pay attention to other people for many reasons other than the tugs of morality. One can love them, be friends with them, be related to them, have a job to look after them, work together in such a way that cooperation and coordination are essential. The idea resurfaces that morality cannot be merely other-directed concern but involves some special domain of issues and concerns or of rules and rationality. Thus we find ourselves in the somewhat peculiar position that while the study of ethics centers on the concept of morality it is precisely that concept which is in question. What is morality? Does morality consist of some special domain? Or could the distinction between moral and nonmoral issues be a bogus distinction, an odd historical curiosity or a merely rhetorical device? Is morality so important, or is it nothing more than an overly precise name for a more general sense of the public good, caring about other people and being a good person.

INTRODUCING KANT

Somewhere near the beginning of any book on ethics, it is virtually compulsory to introduce the most prominent single philosopher in modern ethics, who is, more than anyone else, responsible for this emphasis on morality in ethics, Immanuel Kant. Kant was a German who wrote at the end of the eighteenth century. In ethics, it is Kant who introduces the most distinctive philosophical version of the Golden Rule; it is also Kant, however, who defends the strictest characterization of morality in the history of ethics. His somewhat technical version of the Golden Rule is, "Act so that the maxim (principle) of your action can be willed as universal law." Kant's thesis is a formal version of the demand that morality is essentially universal and that moral principles are universalizable; moral rules always apply to everyone and never refer to just one person or that person's own interests alone. But where most conceptions of morality tend to give equal emphasis to both one's own interests and the interests of others (as in the standard formulations of the Golden Rule), Kant separates self-interest and morality completely; indeed, insofar as an act is based on "inclinations" of any kind (whether personal desires or sympathy for the other fellow), that act is not called "morally worthy." Morality, he says, is a law unto itself, "categorical" and independent of all personal interests and inclinations. Accordingly, Kant analyzes morality in terms of what he calls the "categorical imperative." An imperative, of course, is simply a command; morality for Kant consists of rules. "Categorical" is a strong way of insisting on the absolute nature of moral rules.

According to Kant, morality is thoroughly objective, a product of reason ("practical reason"). A moral principle has nothing to do with personal interest or the particular circumstances of the case. It is thoroughly disinterested, in other words, and it is also what Kant calls *a priori,* or "prior to" any particular cases or moral judgments we might make. It is in Kant's ethics, in other words, that the four basic features of morality are brought together into a singularly powerful conception of morality. Many philosophers and readers have challenged this conception as too narrow, too impersonal, even "heartless," and many others have come to Kant's defense and argued more flexible, less dogmatic interpretations of his ethics. But even in its most rigid expression, Kant's model of morality is so systematic and persuasive that it is impossible to study ethics without coming to grips with it. Indeed, there are ethicists who would say that the study of ethics today is a study of variations and objections to the theory set out by Kant some two hundred years ago. Still others would say that the heart of contemporary ethics is the rejection of this same moral theory.

ETHICS, ETHOS, AND MORALITY: THE PROBLEM OF RELATIVISM

To understand the ethos and the ethics of various peoples is one of the aims of the science of anthropology. Ethics, however, is something more than this. For example, as the great French anthropologist Claude Levi-Strauss commented in a 1970 interview:

> When I witness certain decisions or modes of behavior in my own society, I am filled with indignation and disgust, whereas if I observe similar behavior in a so-called primitive society, I make no attempt at a value judgment. I try to understand it.

Philosophers often distinguish between *descriptive* statements and *prescriptive* statements; the former tell us what the facts are, but the latter tell us what *ought* to be. It is one thing to describe what people do and what they value; it is something more to enter into their lives and tell them what they ought to do and value. In anthropology, we can and should be content with description. In ethics, however, our descriptions are always mixed with prescriptions, for we are not merely trying to understand ourselves. We are also trying to live well and do what is right.

Ethics is not a descriptive science but an active participation in a set of values, a way of life. But as we have already noted the notion of "a way of life" leaves open the question of whether some ways of life (human sacrifice or military aggression for the fun of it) might be morally wrong. Morality, as characterized in the preceding section, is universal and not just one set of values among others. Moral rules, accordingly, get applied not just to one's own ethos, but to all others as well. When European explorers found out that the natives of the New World practiced human sacrifice, they did not simply note it as an anthropological curiosity; they were horrified (even as the Inquisition was systematically killing people in Europe in the name of Christianity). When Northerners visited the Southern states during the years preceding the Civil War, they did not see slavery as a quaint custom or a local necessity; they viewed it as the grossest immorality and a pretext for war. When some rural German philosophers visited the sweatshops of London and Manchester at the beginning of the industrial revolution, they were indignant, and they started fomenting a revolution of a very different kind. Karl Marx was one of them, and, not surprisingly, he formulated his revolutionary manifesto in the universal vocabulary of morality and justice, not just in economic terms.

Moral rules are more than mores and customs because they claim to outline the conditions which *any* society must fulfill, applicable to everyone, everywhere. The moral prohibition on incest, according to some influential anthropologists and biologists, is not only a universal moral rule, but built right into our genes as well. (Partial evidence for this is the prevalence of incest taboos among most animal species, although such inferences from other species to human morality are always to be made with extreme caution.) The moral rule that "thou shalt not steal" seems to be not just a custom common to many societies, but the necessary condition for there being any secure sense of ownership at all. The moral rule that it is wrong to lie seems to be the precondition of anyone's ever believing anyone else. Imagine visiting a city, for example, where most of the directions you receive are lies, as the natives mischievously send you off in this direction and that. After a short time, you will refuse to listen to any directions at all, knowing the odds against their being correct. A society can exist with *some* lying, of course, but it is impossible to imagine a society in which lies would be more than occasional deceptions, presupposing that most people most of the time tell the truth.

Moral rules are considered to be basic rules because they outline the conditions for the very existence of society. Certain moral rules may be of special importance in particular societies. For example, cheating and plagiarism are considered moral transgressions in a college community because they undermine the conditions for a truly competitive, creative community. Violating a contract and refusing to pay one's bills are considered especially serious violations in business because such acts threaten the very existence of the business community. Some moral rules seem to be of special importance in virtually every society: sexual mores and family relationships, for example, have a profound importance in almost every culture, insofar as having babies and raising them is obviously essential to the continuation of the culture.

Although morals are basic to the existence of a society, there is clearly at least a shift if not a dramatic change in morals depending on changing social and economic conditions. For instance, the morality of having children changes dramatically in times of serious overpopulation or underpopulation. Whenever the population seems to be increasing to the breaking point, many people insist that it is immoral to have more than one or two children, even if a family can easily afford them. In societies eager to increase their population, on the other hand, *not* having children is typically considered a moral failing. (In underpopulated ancient Rome, for example, pregnancy was so encouraged that there was not even a word for "contraception"— ironically, a term derived from Latin roots.) Indeed, there are over-populated societies in which even murder is taken less seriously, and the death of hundreds of people from disease and starvation is considered merely a normal part of daily life. Or, to take a more agreeable example: in a society in which there is much to be accomplished (for instance, in colonial America), work becomes a virtue—even an "ethic" unto itself. Just lying back and enjoying life, the "virtue" of some aristocratic and leisurely societies, is recast as laziness, a vice.

These variations in morals from society to society have naturally troubled moralists and ethical philosophers who would like to find a single, universal set of standards which lies at the basis of all societies. Some ethicists avoid this problem by restricting their attention to the moral rules and the logic of moral thinking just in their own society, without even attempting to pass judgment on societies other than their own. Other ethicists consider the variations on a single set of moral rules that are universal. Consider, for example, the various senses of stealing. Aristotle and much of medieval society considered the taking of profits in business transactions a mode of stealing, and Marxist societies regard the very institution of private property as a form of theft. ("Property is theft," wrote a a nineteenth-century French socialist named Proudhon, who was quoted by Marx.) On Wall Street, it is just another day's business to take an entire company away from its unwilling owners (an "unfriendly acquisition"), so long as the buyer is willing to pay for 51 percent of the stock and an expensive team of lawyers and strategists. What counts as "stealing" is often determined by context. In baseball, running unexpectedly from one canvas sack to another counts as stealing a base, but disrupting the game by picking up one of those sacks and running off with it is not. In the face of very different views of what might be called stealing, it would not seem easy to isolate some underlying—if very complicated—universal principle, summarized simply and without qualification as "thou shalt not steal," which applies to medieval life and Marxism, as well as Wall Street and baseball. But one could argue, for instance, that all of these variations are but special instances of the general rule, "Do not take that to which you are not entitled." Of course, one would then, in any particular application of the rule, have to specify what warrants "entitlement." Aristotle accepted the idea of private property and the desirability of wealth, but rejected the legitimacy of exchange for profit. Marx rejected the institution of private ownership and so saw all accumulation of wealth as theft. Stealing a base is a legitimate play in baseball, but disrupting the field by taking the sack is not. So although what counts as stealing may vary from context to context, the underlying moral prohibition remains the same. But then again, could it be that this underlying principle is trivial—saying only that "Wrongful taking is wrong"?

There are ethicists called *relativists*, however, who reject this idea that there are universal moral principles, with or without local variations and contextual qualifications. Relativists argue that morality is indeed *relative* to an ethos and limited to that ethos. "What is moral in India can get a man hanged in France," wrote one eighteenth-century relativist, his conclusion being that morals are nothing but the local customs of a particular community. This conclusion might not upset us if it meant only that certain customs and mores—eating habits and attitudes toward pets, for example—were different in different societies. Nor would it be especially troublesome if it were only a way of reminding us that particular moral rules and actions differ from place to place—whether charging high interest rates counts as "stealing," or whether early abortion counts as "murder." What is upsetting is the idea that cold-blooded murder or slavery might be moral in feudal Japan or ancient Greece, for example, and that we have no right whatever to condemn them.

Relativism in its extreme form claims that there is much more than just superficial differences among societies. It insists that the most basic rules of morality are different too, that not only what counts as murder, for example, but even murder itself has different moral status in different societies. For example, in some cultures, religious sacrifices, such as Agamemnon's slaughter of his daughter and the Aztec annual vivisectionist rituals, were considered legitimate forms of killing. Trying to bridge the cross-cultural gap, one might say that it is not a murder in such cases because there was *some reason* for the killing, namely, a religious reason. But this weak suggestion would eliminate as murder virtually all cases of killing except involuntary manslaughter (which is not murder) and the very rare cases of intentional murder without any (conscious) reason at all. Again, one might make the purely verbal point that murder by definition means "wrongful killing," and thus *all* murder is (necessarily) wrong, but this just moves the question back one step to "killing," and whether killing is always considered wrong.

Relativism continues to be one of the most pressing problems in ethics, and it will follow us like a shadow through many of the discussions in this book. A society's ethos is partially defined and circumscribed by its morals, but does the ethos alone define and circumscribe morals? Is morality, like etiquette and entertainment, just the product of a particular society, or does it underlie the *ethè* of all societies as their basic foundation? Are we justified in extending our moral principles to people across the world? Or is this, too, just another example of "imperialism," the unwanted imposition of one culture's tastes and standards upon another which itself is considered, by many people, to be morally wrong?

EGOISM AND ALTRUISM

Just as some philosophers have been suspicious that what we call "morality" may be only the projection of our own ethics onto other people, many philosophers and a great many other people (e.g., most economists) have suspected (or presumed) that what moves people to act is virtually never morality or the interests of other people (except, perhaps, their closest kin) but rather *one's own* interests, which may or may not coincide with the moral rules. Of course, such behavior in one's own interest need not be crude or inconsiderate, and it need not even serve one's own interests "in the short run." Indeed, the mark of smart or "enlightened" self-interest or what we call *prudence* is precisely the wisdom to be considerate and concerned with the well-being of others if only as a means to furthering one's own long-term interests. Prudence is still self-interest, but it involves caution, social awareness, and long-term thinking. It may be an enormous thrill to drive your car at top speeds down a winding country road, but you could easily be killed or, given the occasional pedestrian loitering in the middle of the road, kill someone. It may be what you want at the moment, but it is not prudent. It may seem to be in your self-interest to cheat on an exam, when that one extra grade will get you on the dean's list. But you may be caught and expelled; you may be initiating a habit that will ruin or deprive your educational talents later on; you will deprive yourself of the opportunity to prove your worth on your own; you will probably lower yourself in your own eyes and in the eyes of any other students who see you. Cheating may be in your immediate self-interest, but it is not at all prudent. Thus prudence, unlike crude, thoughtless self-interest, is often in conformity with the dictates of morality. But is morality motivated by nothing more than prudence, or is prudence—as enlightened self-interest—still something short of truly moral behavior?

One of the most enduring debates in ethics (dating back to Plato, at least) concerns this question of motivation in morals. Do we, in fact, always act for the sake of our self-interest? Or do we, at least sometimes, act for the sake of duty alone, for the sake of others without regard to our own self-interest? Traditionally, this dichotomy between acting out of one's own self-interest versus acting for the benefit of others has been marked by the terms *egoism* and *altruism*. Egoism is acting out of self-interest. Altruism is acting for the benefit of others. Altruism may be based on some sense of attachment or compassion, but it need not be. One could be altruistic on principle, always considering other people's interests as more important than his own. Like many ethical categories, egoism and altruism are used to refer to the consequences as well as the motivation of behavior. Egoism is action that benefits oneself. Altruism is action that benefits others. (Many biologists have even begun using the words egoism and altruism to refer to the behavior of genes, viruses, and one-celled life forms, where the question of motive cannot intelligibly arise.) But the primary meaning of these terms is and must be tied to motivation, not consequences. One can, perhaps despite one's bad intentions, benefit others, but such behavior is not by any means altruistic. One often does, unfortunately, fail in one's efforts to help others, occasionally benefiting oneself in the process. And whether or not genes or genotypes exhibit patterns that can be described as self-perpetuating, "selfishness" is hardly the motive.

On the one hand, egoism is obviously antithetical to morality; it designates concern for one's own interests whatever the rules and whatever one's obligations. (One can, of course, be moral and fulfill obligations just as a means to satisfying one's interests.) On the other hand, many ethicists have argued that egoism is the sole basis for *any* human behavior, moral or otherwise. This raises a very difficult question: if this is true, how is it possible ever to act for the sake of morality (unless our obligations also satisfy our interests)? Are we moral (when we are moral) only because being so is in our interests? If I give money to a beggar and feel good that I have done so, have I in fact given him the money only in order to feel good afterward? This raises the age-old question of "human nature," and whether we are indeed "by nature" selfish creatures or perhaps rather social beings in whom concern for others and at least some minimal sense of compassion is equally natural. But it also raises another debate, which questions not our nature, but rather the strategies we use to get along in life. Then the question is not what we "naturally" feel or do but rather what we *ought*, as rational creatures, to do. The first issue, again, is descriptive—having to do with what sort of beings we are, the second prescriptive—giving us advice on how to behave.

Philosophers accordingly distinguish between psychological egoism and ethical egoism. *Psychological egoism* is the psychological theory that everything that we do, we do for our own interests, whether or not the same act serves other people's interests or moral obligations. *Ethical egoism* is the view that one ought to act in one's own interests. Of course, if psychological egoism is true, one cannot help but act in one's own interests. Nevertheless, the two positions are distinct. One might believe that all people are motivated by their own interests and nevertheless try to make sure that these interests coincide with the common good and morality (for example, by inflicting punishment to offset any personal advantage in wrongdoing). And one might believe that people are not "naturally" out for their own interests, but that they *ought* to be so. Imagine a person who believes, for instance, that most of the damage done in the world is caused by do-gooders who ought to mind their own business. Egoism, by contrast, might seem like virtue.

Altruism might also be divided into two parts: psychological altruism, the theory that people "naturally" act for the benefit of others; and ethical altruism, the view that they *ought* to act for the benefit of others. Many theorists have debated whether *any* of our actions are altruistically motivated, but very few have ever asserted that *all* of them are. The debate, therefore, typically centers on psychological egoism and the question of whether all our actions are self-interested. Ethical altruism quite naturally runs into questions about the motivation of morality. If we are naturally prone to consider the interests of others and the well-being of society then the egoistic question, "Why should I be moral?" loses much of its force. So, too, if reason has its own motivational influence (above and beyond the motivating power of the inclinations, as Kant suggested), then the idea that we always act self-interestedly also loses its initial persuasiveness. It may well be that some of our desires—even our most basic desires—are to be ethical and to help other people when we can. If so, to call the satisfaction of such desires "self-interested" (much less "selfish") is indeed peculiar if not perverse.

A NOTE ON SELFISHNESS

The somewhat technical notion, egoism, is often conflated or confused with the more familiar word "selfishness." But whereas egoism entails reference to self-interest, it does not exclude concern for others (just as altruism does not exclude satisfying one's own interests). Selfishness, on the other hand, implies lack of consideration of (or outright interference with) other people and their interests. It is, therefore, not just the pursuit of self-interest but the inconsiderate, vulgar pursuit of one's own interests.

According to a popular story, President Lincoln was passing a puddle in a carriage when he saw that several piglets were drowning as the mother pig squealed helplessly. He stopped the carriage and saved the piglets. Back on the road, Lincoln's companion asked him whether that act counted as a pure case of altruism; Lincoln replied, "Why, that was the very essence of selfishness. I should have had no peace of mind all day."

The word "egoism" may suggest some antagonism between one's own interests and the interests of others. Nevertheless, one can be an egoist and also be charming, morally correct, and even a philanthropist, as a number of very wealthy and ambitious people have demonstrated.

The word "selfishness," however, is another matter. Selfishness has built into it the antagonism between one's own and others' interests, and to say that someone is selfish is to say that this person not only is an egoist, but also that he or she subverts the interests of others. Selfishness has an undeniable connotation of condemnation and should not be confused with the more neutral term egoism. To suggest that everyone's behavior is motivated by self-interest is at least a plausible hypothesis; to suggest that everyone's behavior is selfish is both offensive and implausible (though nevertheless there are terrible times when it appears to be true). Accordingly, Lincoln's reply to his friend is a bit of playful nonsense. Satisfying oneself is not the same as being selfish, and even if most human action is (at least in part) self-interested, it is not therefore selfish as well.

WHY BE MORAL? SELF-INTEREST, MOTIVATION, AND JUSTIFICATION

Many of the problems that arise in our thinking about morality are the product of an overly sharp dichotomy between the demands of morality and self-interest. Morality is said to be "disinterested," while self-interest is obviously "interested." Moral rules have some sort of universality and apply to everyone, but self-interest is distinctively particular and concerned with a single person, oneself. (Matters become curiously complicated when self-interest is turned into pseudo-moral doctrine, as in "everyone *ought* to pursue his or her own self-interest." But this is usually argued just on the (dubious) grounds that, *if* everyone were to pursue his or her own self-interest, then the results would be best *for everyone*—and so it turns out not to be an ethics of self-interest after all.) We have already noted that the sharp opposition between morality and self-interest leads to a problem of motivation, namely, *if* it is true that people do only what they want to do and act only according to their own interests, then why (for what reason, by virtue of what motive) could or should people ever act *against* their interests, as morality may sometimes require? In our opening example, why should one pay back a debt just because morality demands it? An apostle of self-interest might point to our opening story and insist that the reason for repaying the debt was not the sense of obligation (which would be a distinctively moral motive) but rather the personal pain of guilt and the annoyance of those nagging thoughts. Or it may have been with an eye to future possible loans. In other words, despite any noble appearances, the act was self-interested. Indeed, the apostle might say, *all* actions, no matter how moral or heroic or apparently generous, are motivated by self-interest. We may continue to distinguish, the apostle might allow, between moral appearances and self-interest, but we should understand that all actions are ultimately self-interested.

This sharp opposition between morality and self-interest also has dangerous implications. In a society that preaches the virtues of self-reliance and "looking out for number one," the allure of self-interest becomes more than a perverse theory of moral motivation; it becomes a *rationale* for selfish and immoral behavior as well. In our opening scenario, this view had its explosive but short-lived expression in the table-bashing declaration, "The only person I have to worry about is me!" But in the competitive world of business and professional careers, as well as the all's-fair worlds of professional sports, love, and war, this rationale can lead to outright rejection of moral rules, and the world really can become, in the words of the seventeenth-century philosopher Thomas Hobbes, "a war of all against all" in which life becomes "nasty, brutish, and short." It is a world summarized, too, in a popular version of Darwinism, as a "jungle" in which the only rule is "survival of the fittest."

It is a mistake, however, to present the opposition between morality and self-interest as an inevitable conflict. Most of the time, because of shared and mutual interests, because of considerations of reputation, because of the threat of punishment, or because of painful pangs of conscience, our interests coincide with our moral obligations. And indeed, if they did not, we could rearrange society, with systematic rewards and more rigorous, efficient punishment, in such a way that individual interests would almost always coincide with social and moral principles. But this could be a Draconian measure, and it already assumes that people are basically self-interested and will cooperate and obey the rules only if they are, essentially, forced to do so. A much more amiable suggestion is that people are naturally social and sociable and are prone to behave in whatever ways are admirable or acceptable in their society. They tend to be selfish and act in their own self-interest (to the obvious detriment of others) only when they are taught or forced to do so, by an excessive emphasis on competition to the detriment of cooperation, by conditions of scarcity or adversity that make cooperation impossible. But even then, one should note, people in extreme emergency conditions often act with great courage and generosity. They do not become more antagonistic, but more cooperative.

The idea that people are naturally self-interested, antagonistic, and accept moral constraints only when forced to do so seems to give us a false picture of human nature, and so too a false picture of morality.

We can imagine a world in which moral action and self-interest would always agree, if society were arranged so that people were rewarded for doing beneficial and socially productive deeds, if they were thoroughly socialized as members of the community and educated in civic participation and, where this failed, the penalties were such that immoral or antisocial action would always be against one's better self-interests. This would still not eliminate the distinction between morality and self-interest, however, and one still might insist that the behavior in question, however much in *accordance* with morality, nonetheless fell short of moral behavior. On a very strict (Kantian) moral point of view, to be moral requires the intention to be moral "for its own sake," and this entails at least minimal resistance to one's inclinations. And, of course, it is not moral if one wants only to reap rewards or avoid punishments or censure. To tell the truth because one is afraid of being punished for lying does not strike us as morally worthy. Thus, the motivation of morality is not only a matter of getting people to behave morally; it is also an essential ingredient in morality. To borrow Kant's much-quoted example, a grocer who doesn't cheat his customers just because he is afraid of getting caught cannot be counted as a moral example. He is concerned only with staying in business.

The extent to which an action is self-interested gives us a ready understanding of its motivation, but a distinctively moral action seems to require something more than self-interest. Thus Kant tells us that an action has "moral worth" only insofar as it is motivated by duty alone. The motivation of morality thus becomes a key question in ethics, a matter of extreme practical, as well as theoretical, importance. The question of motivation leads quickly into the larger question of *justification*. If moral actions are not (entirely) self-interested, what reasons and arguments can we give for the moral thesis that people ought sometimes to act against their own self-interest? The simple question, "Why be moral?" summarizes both these issues. On the one hand, it can be construed as the query, "How is it in my interest to be moral?" On the other hand, it is the more general question of how ought-type rules can be rationally supported, even in the absence of self-interest.

The problem of justification is to show the ultimate *correctness* of our moral rules. Minimally, the justification of an action is a demonstration that it is (was) the best thing to do in a certain set of circumstances. Ideally, such a demonstration would also show that it was the objectively right thing to do, backed up by the right reasons. One part of the justification of an act might be its contribution to self-interest, and we might also be encouraged by learning that other people did or would have done the same thing, but neither of these is sufficient as justification. Self-interested acts are justified only if they do not violate certain moral constraints, for example, respect for the rights of others, and we all recognize that "everyone is doing it" is usually a pretty pathetic excuse if the action in question is clearly wrong. But what more do we need to justify an action?

The most obvious answer is the existence of some moral rule that permits or commands one kind of action and forbids or prohibits others. One might point out that one has a duty or an obligation. Another kind of justification will be that the action benefits as many people and harms as few as possible. Still another will point out that one course of action (as opposed to any number of others) is fair, or at least, as close to fair as possible. Notice that all of these attempts at justification appeal to some form of objectivity—a moral rule, an obligation, a measurable difference in benefits and harms, some standard of fairness (such as, "each person should get the same" or "each person should get what he or she deserves").

There are, however, people who would argue that moral rules, measurements of help and harm and standards for fairness, are never really objective—even if they are presented as such. Thus we meet the *moral skeptic,* who doubts that any ethical code can be justified. To the skeptic, all morality is ultimately arbitrary, convenient, perhaps, and appropriately "relative" to different societies. But it cannot be justified and cannot be shown to be objectively correct or defensible by dispassionate reason. Thus David Hume, one of the great moral skeptics, argued that morality was just a matter of "sentiments," some of which were universal and "natural," but they were not rational and not rationally justifiable. But Hume, we should note, was a perfect gentleman of his time, and the fact that he thought morality to be unjustifiable did not seem to affect his behavior at all. The moral skeptic doubts or denies the possibility of justification, but accepts morality nonetheless. A more dangerous character is the *amoralist,* a person who acts without regard for generally accepted moral principles, and worse yet is the *immoralist,* who recognizes those principles but conscientiously disobeys them. Both the amoralist and the immoralist are sometimes called "nihilists," who do not only deny the justifiability of morality but refuse to accept its dictates as well. Happily, however, very few people are either amoralists or immoralists, and nihilism is more often a roguish pose than a genuine philosophy. But the very possibility of nihilism has provoked philosophers to pursue their quest for an adequate justification of morality, or, at least, for an account of moral behavior that assures us that ethics is indeed a genuine motive for human behavior.

REASON AND THE EMOTIONS

David Hume, although a skeptic with regard to morality, argued that ethics was a matter of emotion, or of what he called the *passions*. In particular, he appealed to the moral sentiments, those relatively calm emotions that tie us to other people and make us care for and about them. Hume went so far as to argue that "reason is, and ought to be, the slave of the passions," and he argued that morals are not rationally justifiable. Nevertheless, Hume insisted that morals were based on the moral sentiments, and thus one might take him to be proffering a different kind of justification, a different kind of reason, a feeling. Hume thought that at least some moral sentiments, notably sympathy, were universal and "natural." But might not this be enough for ethics to be both rational and rationally justifiable? Ethics and morality are not just about principles and reasons. We are also motivated by our emotions, and these emotions themselves may be or may provide good reasons. They may thus supply an important mode of justification. "Because I love her" and "because I feel sorry for him" are certainly good reasons for helping someone, and in the absence of contrary reasons and arguments these would seem like sound justifications for action. If one were to save the life of a homicidal maniac, only to have him go on to kill several innocent people, feeling sorry for him would not be good enough. But in the absence of such considerations, say, if it is a lost child needing help finding his way home, "because I felt sorry for him" would be a perfectly good reason and probably more convincing than "because I felt that I had a duty to help him" or "because it will decrease the amount of suffering in the world."

The role of the emotions in ethics has often been underestimated, or even denied. Many people use "emotional" as a synonym for "irrational" or think of the emotions only in terms of uncontrollable fear or anger and conclude too quickly that emotions can only get in the way of ethical behavior. But Aristotle, as we will see, defines many of the virtues in terms of their constituent emotions, for instance, when he defines courage as the "mean between the extremes" of having too much and having too little fear. Moral education thus includes the cultivation of the emotions, or what Aristotle called the "passions" (*pathê*). Doing the right thing also involves having the right passions, at the right time, in the right amount, appropriate for the situation. Anger, for example, is not always an inappropriate emotion. Aristotle notes that in the face of a serious offense or slight (possibly to one's friends), a person would be a fool not to get angry. Thus having a good temper requires the cultivation of anger, not the simple elimination or control of it, but its appropriateness in all sorts of situations.

Hume's moral sentiment theory focuses perhaps too much on such feelings as sympathy, to the neglect of reason and reasoning. But concern with feelings, or more accurately, the emotions, is by no means unique to moral sentiment theory. Kant gives more attention than is often supposed to the "inclinations" (emotions, desires, moods, and such) and he has a high estimation of compassion, even if he does not think that, as an inclination, it has that special feature that he calls moral worth. Utilitarians, of course, have to take feelings into account in their utility calculations. If a course of action hurts a lot of people's feelings, then that is a good reason not to undertake that course of action. If an action makes a lot of people happy, then that is a good reason for endorsing that action. Notice, in these examples, that the feelings and emotions are included in the consequences of the action rather than their motivation, but the feelings and emotions that motivate behavior must also be taken into account. Giving generously because one enjoys being generous adds to the overall happiness in the world. In addition to being a virtue, it thus also maximizes utility. So, in a sense, the utilitarians are also moral sentiment theorists in that they take at least some emotions to be important in ethics. We might note that the moral sentiment theorists also tended to be utilitarian.

David Hume was perhaps the best-known of the moral sentiment theorists. There was also Jean-Jacques Rousseau, the famous Swiss philosopher of "the noble savage," and Adam Smith, better known as the father of modern economics. Moral sentiment theory insists that emotions (or what in the eighteenth century were usually referred to as "the passions") are essential to ethics. Sympathy and compassion, in particular, were considered important both as "springs of action" and as essential attributes of a good person. In his *Theory of the Moral Sentiments,* Adam Smith wrote:

> How selfish so ever man may be supposed, there are evidently some principles in his nature, which interest him in the fortune

of others, and render their happiness necessary to him, though he derives nothing from it except the pleasure of seeing it. Of this kind is pity or compassion, the emotion which we feel for the misery of others. . . . The greatest ruffian, the most hardened violator of the laws of society, is not altogether without it.

Smith and Hume defended the importance of other sentiments as well, for instance the passion of pride (which in medieval philosophy had been considered a "deadly" sin) and the personal virtue of justice (although Hume added that this was not a natural but an acquired virtue). It was such celebratory accounts of the moral sentiments that Kant rejected, when he insisted that morality could not depend on the inclinations, but even he acknowledged that there was something beautiful about compassion. Kant worried that the moral sentiments were too idiosyncratic, too capricious, to provide a secure basis for ethics, but this is just what the moral sentiment theorists who preceded him denied by insisting that these were "natural," and therefore universal, passions. Even Hume worried, however, that these moral sentiments seriously diminished with distance, so that one might easily feel sympathy for one's brother or neighbor, but might well feel virtually nothing at all for some distant foreigner whom one never met face to face.

The moral sentiment theorists insisted that the basis of morality and justice is to be found in our natural disposition to have other-directed sentiments and passions that maintain our own self-respect and self-esteem. But the debate between reasons and passions, principles and inclinations, should not be overplayed. We often criticize people's passions and sentiments if they are irrational, inappropriate, or wrong-headed. In other words, we apply standards of rationality to the emotions as well as to principles and other reasons for action. So talking about the moral sentiments does not mean that morality is not, in part, a function of reason or, above all, a matter of "doing the right thing." But the right things don't usually get done for the wrong reasons, and we don't usually think of ourselves or of others as just or moral if the right thing gets done for the wrong reasons or if the wrong thing gets done for the right reasons. But surely among the right reasons are the sympathetic emotions such as helping another person in need because "I feel sorry for him." Indeed, one is hard put to think of any other reason that is so persuasive.

What seems to be reasonable to say is that ethics involves feeling as well as reason and reasoning. Feelings (or more accurately, emotions,

passions, and sentiments) without critical thinking and careful deliberation, often aided by general principles, may be misleading, naïve,
and sometimes dangerous. On the other hand, reason and reasoning
need something to reason about, and that begins with the fact that we
care about other people, we care about ourselves and our own sense
of dignity or self-respect, and we care about our values. Moral sentiment theory rightly captured one aspect of ethics, but Kant and his
colleagues captured another.

ACTING FOR REASONS

The key to morality and its justification is that we do not just act, we
act for *reasons.* Indeed, it is the very nature of human action that it is
intentional, which means that it is (1) purposive and (2) done for reasons. Whether or not we have an intention in mind before acting (an
articulate thought concerning what we are going to do), our actions
are nevertheless intentional. To say that our actions are rational is, minimally, to say that they have an intelligible purpose, and this purpose
can (usually) be stated more or less clearly and without hesitation as a
reason for action. Only in the exceptional case do we have to ponder
the difficult question, "Why did I do that? (Under the prodding of a
psychoanalyst or philosopher, of course, one might well become confused about his or her motivation for even the most ordinary actions.
But usually our reasons for action are transparent even if they usually
remain unstated.)

Dogs can act with a purpose, of course. Fido scratches at the screen
door *in order to* attract attention and be let out. But dogs don't act for
reasons in the sense that is relevant to ethics, and, accordingly, even the
best-behaved dog does not deserve to be called moral. It is not just
that reasons in ethics should be articulate, thus requiring language.
(This traditional criterion for distinguishing between man and beast
may well be both unfair and false.) It is, rather, that reasons require
reason, which is to say, a complex of reasons beyond the immediate
"do this to get that." Reasoning requires abstractions, reflection, and
the need to justify one's course of action. A college woman with the
ambition to be a federal judge someday has to think in terms of years
or decades, not just in terms of wanting to get into law school (in the
sense in which someone's pet dog at the door of the law building
"wants to get into the law school"). She has to think in terms of her

education, her credentials, her reputation, her choice of friends, the way she will spend her summers. And, to state the obvious, she must have a concept of the law and the legal system, which would not be comprehensible to even the brightest German shepherd dog.

There is nothing in this complex of reasons that need be particularly moral, of course. Indeed, the young woman's ambition may have wholly to do with her own vision of herself, perhaps "to show them" back in Wichita Falls. But such an ambition is a clear example of how conceptually rich it is to act intentionally, to act for reasons. Indeed, even grabbing a Big Mac in the local fast-food lane has conceptual richness, and so the question, "For what reason?" is appropriate (though the predictable answer, "Because I'm hungry," is only the beginning of an adequate account). To act for reasons means that the question of justification is relevant and important. It is not just an annoying addendum that philosophers have added to human action; it is part and parcel of human action as such. We would be shocked, to say the least, if the question, "Why do you want to go to law school?" were answered simply by, "Oh, I have no idea whatever" or "It just sounds like fun." Actions have reasons, and these reasons in turn have reasons. One applies to law school to get into law school, which one does in order to become a lawyer, which one does in order, perhaps, to enter politics, make money, join one's mother's law firm, etc. Ethics, then, can be considered the study of our reasons.

Reasoning and justification must have an end, however. There must be a terminus, a final purpose, or what the ancient Greeks (notably Aristotle) called a *telos*. A chain of reasons needs to be anchored; the network of reasons has to be hung somewhere. One might say, for example, that the ultimate reason for going to law school—or for doing anything, for that matter—is to be happy. Or to get more pleasure out of life. Or to become as powerful or as popular as possible. Such final ends provide the end of our reasoning. Indeed, if the skeptic returns with another unreasonable question, such as "Why do you want to be happy?" we seem stuck for an answer. Perhaps we can mumble something like "It's just human nature to want to be happy" or "Well, everyone wants to be happy." But, again, we have the feeling that the question is unreasonable. One does not, after all, question ultimate ends—and certainly not happiness.

The above candidates for the position of ultimate end of action and anchor for our reasons are, whatever their differences, all of a kind. They are all ultimate *purposes,* desirable ends in themselves toward which all our other actions and reasons are aimed. But there is another

31

kind of reason, and another kind of terminus to our reasoning. The most prominent example, in our context, is "Because it is the right thing to do." Also, "Because it is my duty to do so." "Because God wills it" is still another. How are these reasons different from those mentioned previously? For one thing, ethicists would point out that they are not *personal* reasons in the way that happiness, pleasure, popularity, and power are; they specify considerations that are independent of people's wants or desires. They are *moral* reasons, that is, they already presuppose the vocabulary and the viewpoint of the language of right and wrong, good and evil, moral and immoral, ought and obligation. It is evident that such reasons are involved in many of our actions, whether or not we are called upon to justify ourselves. That fact is not challenged even by the moral skeptic, who would agree that we (and most cultures) employ such reasons and act according to them. The skeptical challenge is rather aimed at the ultimate justification of such reasons, that is, the idea that the chain of moral reasons can be anchored in some objective truth or principle.

We have noted that the same question can be asked of the personal purposes above, as in "Why do you want to be happy?" But the moral skeptic—and most of us—would be quite willing to continue in the quest for happiness, or perhaps even pleasure, or popularity, or power, even if he or she were not convinced that there were any more ultimate purpose in doing so. But this is not so clear where morality itself is the end. We are moral, presumably, because we assume that there is some higher reason for being so than our own personal well-being. If morality is unjustifiable in either of these senses, there may indeed be no answer to the unreasonable question, "Why be moral?"

The quest for justification is answered by *theories* of morality. A moral theory is not just an attempt to describe or explain the phenomenon of morality (as a theory in the natural or social sciences would). It is an attempt to justify morality, to provide the anchor for moral reasons. Using a different metaphor, many philosophers—especially Kant—would speak of "grounding" morality, building a rational foundation upon which all our reasons can then be combined in a single coherent structure. But, as we have noted above two different kinds of reasons and two different kinds of "anchors" or "groundings," so too we have two different kinds of theories of morality corresponding to the two senses of justification. (In addition, perhaps, to the grounding of morality in the moral sentiments, a la Hume.) Morality may be justified by showing that it has its own moral terminus; the ultimate reason is more fundamental than any personal or collective

goals we might have, including happiness. Or morality may be justified by showing that it leads, ultimately, to the attainment of personal
and collective goals, such as happiness. But, in this latter case, moral
reasons are not themselves the ultimate reasons. Morality is a means to
something else, such as happiness or social well-being.

Moral philosophers have traditionally given two rather formidable
names to these two kinds of theories. Theories of morality which claim
that morality provides its own ultimate anchor or grounding are called
deontological (from the Greek word *deon,* or "duty"). Theories of morality which place some nonmoral purpose at the end of moral reasoning
are called *teleological* (from the Greek word *telos,* or "purpose"). We will
examine several varieties of these theories in the following chapter.

RULES AND VIRTUES

In our introduction to ethics, we have so far followed an established
Kantian tradition by placing a special emphasis on *morality.*
Accordingly, we have been emphasizing the importance of *moral principles* in ethics, and, indeed, our ethical tradition is built around the
importance of formally stated rules, from the Ten Commandments in
the Old Testament to the policy of "government by laws, not men,"
put into practice by the framers of the United States Constitution.
But this emphasis on principles is not the whole of ethics, and there
are many systems of ethics that do not place such stress on principles
at all. We have already noted moral sentiment theory, which would
reject the emphasis on moral principles in favor of grounding morality in the moral sentiments. Then there are societies where the central
concern of ethics is obedience—to a ruler or a religious leader, for
example—and general principles of the sort we have been discussing
may not enter into their system of ethics. One could always formulate
the principle, "Do whatever he or she says!" but this is a dubious
example of a moral principle. The nature of ethics as well as its specific content is also a matter of ethos, and not all ethè are so bound up
with what we call morality.

What is essential to ethics might not be universal rules and objective
rational principles, but rather an established way of doing things, a
shared sense of value and significance. Consider a group of children at
play, throwing a ball or chasing through the woods. Their game does not
necessarily need rules. In fact, one might suggest, they tend to formulate

rules for activities only when things start to get out of hand. For example, one of the children may decide to sit on the ball and not let the others have it. Consequently the others formulate a "no-sitting-on-the-ball" rule. What is essential for understanding almost all human activities is not so much the notion of a rule as such as it is the idea of a *practice,* a shared cooperative activity with mutually understood goals and ways of doing things. Most practices have rules, but rules are not what define the practice. Consider, for example, almost any game. Games are paradigmatic practices. The object of a game may be as simple as keeping a ball in motion or as complicated as the trading games that are daily played on Wall Street. Every game has its characteristic activities—batting, kicking, running, tackling, checkmating—and its essential equipment—a ball of a certain shape, distinctive pieces on a checkered board. Every game distinguishes behavior that is unacceptable and punishable, and every game has its rituals, its ways of doing things, some of which are specified in the rules and dictated by the very purpose of the game. Others just grow up with the game as part of its traditions. Most games have their champions, whom both players and spectators admire. So, too, a society will inevitably have its goals, perhaps the happiness and prosperity of all of its citizens, but perhaps alternatively sheer military might, prestige, or religious orthodoxy, whether such goals are conducive to happiness and prosperity or not. A society will have its characteristic activities and rituals, only some of which are essential to survival as such, and it will have its heroes and idols, whom the citizens will emulate: a self-made millionaire in a primarily business society, a warrior-chieftain in a primarily military society, a spiritual leader in a primarily religious society. It is sometimes suggested that many social activities work best without formal rules or laws. Thus, business people decry government regulation and insist that the business world works best when left to its own nonmoral governance by supply and demand. And artists often insist that their art consists more in defiance of convention than in obedience to a set of rules. In fact, strict obedience to a set of rules (e.g., in paint-by-numbers paintings) sometimes produces the very worst "art" imaginable. What is important is the practice and its traditions, and, of course, the talents and effort of the individuals participating.

In our preliminary characterization of morality, we said that many theorists would insist that morality consists of rules, principles, and laws; it is not merely right action but right action *on principle.* If we were to accept this as a characterization of ethics, we might have to conclude that many of our activities are devoid of ethical concern, that is, if they are not circumscribed and defined by some set of explicit moral principles. In business, for example, there are any number of implicit understandings about what is fair and what is not, and a great deal of business goes on by way of merely verbal agreements or just a handshake, mutual trust, and understanding. (This is what is so misleading about the popular characterization of business as unethical because it is based solely on "the profit motive." In fact, business is more like a complex game in which the sense of mutual participation and cooperation is presupposed just as much as the much-celebrated spirit of competition.) Many societies are based on ritual, tradition, and obedience to authority, and there is much to their ethics that is not necessarily a matter of principle.

We do not want to say that such activities are amoral. Instead, we are more likely to expand our sense of morals. Or we might insist instead that morality is not all there is to ethics. The ancient Greeks, for instance, would not have understood our emphasis on rules and principles. They were far more concerned with the *character* of individuals and their distinctive *virtues*. Obeying the laws of society was more or less taken for granted, but a good person was not just someone who obeyed the rules. Such people also displayed personal traits and exceptional abilities, characteristics which involved much more than simply abstaining from evil. Indeed, a Homeric Greek with many warrior virtues might indulge in a great many evils and nevertheless remain an ethical hero. Greek ethics turned on individual virtue and heroism more than on obedience and principled behavior.

Largely because of the influence of the great German philosopher Immanuel Kant, however, the emphasis in ethics in the past two hundred years has been on the specific nature of morality as a set of universal principles. But, although we might expect to find rules of some kind in any articulate civilization, it would be a mistake to think of rules alone as the key to ethics. Ethics concerns character and the characteristics of particular individuals rather than rules and obedience. For example, the virtues of compassion, generosity, courage, and so on are an important part of morals, but they do not consist in following rules. Moral behavior in this sense is often spontaneous, habitual, "without thinking," while morality in the Kantian sense places a premium on being deliberative, thoughtful, and reflective. This emphasis on character also allows us to focus on what is special about a person, his or her particular virtues. There is no reason to expect that all admirable people will be the same.

This shift from morality as obedience of a specific set of rules to character has its problematic aspects. For instance, there is some question

whether an ethics of character can provide anything like a decision procedure for making ethical choices. And there are questions as to what
standards character is to be evaluated. For example, one of the more
interesting complications of the introduction of the virtues into ethics is
the complicated moral status of people who don't obey the rules but
nevertheless emerge as heroes of a sort. One notably problematic example is the *rogue*. Some rogues—Robin Hood, for instance—might be
morally defended as appealing to a higher morality than the laws of the
land. But many of the heroes in American movies, for example, have no
such thought in mind. They may simply be asserting their own freedom
or having a good time. They are chased by the police, and they do such
things as wreck cars and rob banks. They even betray their friends, yet
they retain our admiration because of the characters they are. On the
more respectable side of the law, too, we find general admiration for the
rogue. For example, one of our heroes today is the *entrepreneur*, the type
of maverick businessman who takes high risks in order to get a new idea
or product on the market. The entrepreneur too is a rogue. One professor at the Harvard Business School recently wrote that to understand the
entrepreneur, you have to understand the mind of a juvenile delinquent.
Many of our most popular artists and musicians are admired despite what
would seem to be their dubious morals. So the question, "What virtues
are to count?" becomes central to the issue of virtue ethics. Are there
specifically *moral* virtues, and if so, could it be that virtue ethics is nothing but morality in action—moral rules internalized and cultivated as
habit? Then the distinction between two kinds of ethics collapses and
morality retains its central place. Or is virtue something more than
morality and quite different in kind? But first, we should look much
closer at the institution of morality itself, its nature and justification.

APPENDIX:
TEN GREAT MORAL PHILOSOPHERS

Our ethics as well as our ethos is derived from a long tradition,
stretching back in history to ancient times. Foremost among the books
and authors that have influenced us, of course, are the Bible and its
many scribes and speakers. But of nearly equal importance are the
mores and opinions of the ancient peoples of Greece and Rome as
well as dozens of other ethnic groups whose views on life have slowly
evolved into our own.

In philosophy, however, the history of ethics is punctuated, if not actually defined by a number of truly great moral philosophers who wrote about the mores and morals of their own societies and, at the same time, tried to say something universal about morality and living the good life. Even a survey of the history of ethics would include several dozen such authors, and a detailed study would take many years and include possibly hundreds or thousands of minor moralists, essayists, theologians, social reformers, political theorists, and newspaper editors. But for our purposes here, we will find that several names have repeatedly appeared in our discussion and will continue to do so for the remainder of the book. Accordingly, what follows is a brief introduction to ten of the most influential moral philosophers in Western history:

Socrates and Plato

Aristotle

Saint Augustine

Thomas Hobbes

David Hume

Immanuel Kant

John Stuart Mill

Friedrich Nietzsche

Jean-Paul Sartre

Socrates and Plato

Socrates lived from 470 until 399 BC. His student Plato lived from 427 to 347 BC. Most of what we know of Socrates's ethical teachings comes to us through Plato's writings, in which Socrates's conversations or "dialogues" with other Greek philosophers are preserved in vivid, dramatic form. In Plato's earliest dialogues, Socrates's story and his teachings are carefully preserved for us. Against the Sophists who taught such pessimistic theses as "all men are selfish" and "there is no such thing as justice," Socrates took a positive and optimistic view, exemplifying his own integrity and arguing against injustice. Of particular importance is Socrates's insistence on dialogue and debate, "the examined life," as he called it. Socrates spent his life arguing the importance of living virtuously. In his early seventies, he was accused of "corrupting the youth" with his teaching. He was tried and executed. After his death, Plato established the Academy in Athens for the purpose of continuing Socrates's work. In Plato's later dialogues, he clearly embellished Socrates's views and insisted that, over and above the changing things of this world, there was a pure world of "Forms," including the pure Forms of Justice and the Good.

Aristotle

Aristotle was born in 384 BC in northern Greece. His father was the physician of King Philip of Macedonia, and Aristotle later became tutor to the king's son, Alexander (soon to become "the Great"). Aristotle studied with Plato for eighteen years, but he also became the world's most accomplished scientist. His theories of biology and physics ruled Western science for almost two thousand years. In ethics, he developed a theory that was very much in the spirit of biology. Everything, including all human activity, he argued, has a purpose, a function, a *telos*. The ultimate human purpose is *happiness,* but happiness is not just a life filled with pleasures and satisfactions. It must also be a rational life, a life in accordance with *reason*. And it must be an active and a virtuous life, "a life of rational activity in accordance with virtue."

Saint Augustine

Augustine was born in Africa in 354 AD. He was not religious as a young man but, in his thirties, while in Rome, he embraced Christianity and became one of the most influential voices in the development of Christian ethics and theology. Following Plato's and Socrates's vision of the "pure Form of the Good"—which he interpreted as God— Augustine argued that Christian ethics requires the separation of the secular and the divine. In opposition to Aristotle, Augustine insisted that the purpose of life is religious faith and salvation.

Thomas Hobbes

Hobbes was born in England in 1588. He graduated from Oxford University and entered into a lifetime of study in mathematics, philosophy, and science (one of his friends was Galileo). His philosophical writings were politically controversial and got him into trouble. He escaped to France, but his irreligious writings got him in even more trouble there, and he fled back to England, where he wrote his greatest book, *The Leviathan*. The book is a masterful political treatise in which Hobbes attacks the ancient idea of "the divine right of kings" and replaces it with the radical view that societies are based on a "social contract" between everyone in the society. At the basis of this theory, however, Hobbes also argues his famous thesis that all men are naturally selfish and that, in the "state of nature"—before men enter into the social contract—human life is "nasty, brutish and short," "a war of all against all."

David Hume

Hume was born in Scotland in 1711. He was an atheist and a self-proclaimed "pagan" whose theory of human nature was an attempt to return to the ethics of the Greeks, Aristotle in particular, in which happiness and social utility were of the greatest importance. Accordingly, he attacked Christian virtues, such as humility, which he thought to be degrading. He emphasized the importance of having a virtuous *character,* which includes the "natural" feeling or sentiment of *sympathy* and forms the basis of all ethics. He was skeptical about the traditional emphasis on reason in ethics, suggesting that, "Reason is and ought to be the slave of the passions." Because of his atheism and skepticism, Hume was never able to teach philosophy in the universities, and some of his books were condemned.

Immanuel Kant

Kant was born in eastern Prussia in 1724. He was a pious Lutheran, and his ethical philosophy reflects his Christian sense of morality. The key to his thinking about ethics is that morality is essentially a matter of *practical reason*, and *universal law,* or what he calls the *categorical imperative.* Kant rejected both the idea that moral principles can be securely based on human feelings or "sentiments," and the idea that morals may differ from one society or one time to another. Despite his moral conservatism, however, he remained an ardent enthusiast of the French Revolution of 1789, even through its worst years. And in his great philosophical works, especially three monumental books called *Critiques (The Critique of Pure Reason, The Critique of Practical Reason,* and *The Critique of Judgment),* he set in motion his own powerful revolution in philosophy.

John Stuart Mill

John Stuart Mill was born in 1806 in England. His father, James, was already a famous philosopher who, with Jeremy Bentham, founded the ethical movement known as *utilitarianism.* John Stuart Mill became the movement's most articulate and best-known defender. Utilitarianism is essentially the thesis that a "good" act is that which results in "the greatest good for the greatest number" of people. It is an ethics that, as the name implies, puts its emphasis on the usefulness or utility of actions in making people happy, or at least in not making them more miserable. It is a set of ethics that places far more emphasis on the good or bad *consequences* of an action than it does on the intentions according to which it is carried out. Thus, Mill and Kant are often cast as the central opponents in many contemporary arguments in ethics.

Friedrich Nietzsche

Nietzsche was born in 1844 in a small town in Germany. He spent most of his life, however, in Italy and Switzerland, and he liked to call himself a "good European." He was trained in the classics and loved the life of the ancient Greeks, which he compared unflatteringly with nineteenth-century life. Accordingly, his ethical philosophy consists mainly of a virulent attack on Judeo-Christian morality and its religious supports. He proclaimed that "God is dead" (that is, people no longer believed in Him) and that, given that ominous fact, the morals of our society would soon collapse as well. What we call morality, Nietzsche argued, is in fact just a weapon of the weak that is used to bring everyone to the same level. Unlike most modern moralists, Nietzsche was an unabashed *elitist,* insisting that all people are *not* equal. Some people are superior, and rather than follow the rules of the "herd" they should "follow our virtues." His ethics, according to his imaginary spokesman Zarathustra, is "for a few," for those who find themselves unhealthily inhibited by the strictures of morality and who have much more to offer the world than mere good citizenship.

Jean-Paul Sartre

Sartre was born in Paris in 1905. He is generally recognized as the definitive spokesperson for the philosophy known as *existentialism,* which he expounded in his mammoth wartime work *Being and Nothingness,* which he began while he was in a German prison camp. The central theme of his ethics is the concept of *freedom.* "We are condemned to be free," he writes in his usual dramatic manner. He rejects such ideas as our "natural" purpose is happiness or that we are "naturally" selfish. There is no human nature, except for the fact of our freedom. We are what we *make* of ourselves, Sartre argues, and by the same reasoning, there are no moral laws or principles of reason which bind us all. Our morals are what we *decide* to do, and our principles are those which we *choose* to act upon. In accordance with this philosophy, Sartre was an ardent political reformer, committed to many radical causes before he died in 1980.

2

Doing the Right Thing: The Nature of Morality

From a practical point of view, ethics might simply be summarized as "doing the right thing." Even before we begin to think about theories or the enormous variety of examples and questionable cases that are suggested by "doing the right thing," we all feel quite comfortable with the basic idea. If you make a promise, you ought to keep it. If you borrow money, you ought to return it. If you are reporting on a situation, you ought to tell the truth. If you are taking a test, you ought not to cheat. And so on. Ethics begins, as Aristotle told us, with a good upbringing, and much of this upbringing consists of being taught, in hundreds if not thousands of particular cases, what is the right thing (and what is the wrong thing) to do. But these lessons are not all of equal importance or of the same kind. There is a difference between being taught a nuance of courtesy and being told not to hurt other people. There is a difference between being taught something "for your own good" and being told to do something because it is your duty or an obligation. And it is in the attempt to understand these differences that ethics and education in ethics moves from a collection of cultivated behavioral responses to an understanding of the underlying principles and practices of morality.

What makes such understanding necessary, in part, is the fact that we often find ourselves in situations in which what we have been taught is not sufficient, either because the situation is new to us, because we do not know how to predict the consequences, because it lies in a "grey area" in which it is not evident which of several responses is appropriate, or because it involves an actual conflict between two (or more) very different responses. For example, we are told to tell the truth in response to a query, and we are taught not to hurt people if it can be avoided. But the conjunction of these two sometimes leads to a contradiction, when, for example, answering a query truthfully will result in harm that might otherwise be avoided. (A simple case: a friend who has just gotten a ghastly haircut asks you, "How do I look?" Much more serious, the leader of a lynch mob asks you if you know where your (falsely accused) friend is hiding.) The possibility of novel situations requires some general guidelines which go beyond the limited number of contexts in which one has been ethically educated, and the frequency of "grey areas" requires the ability to reason about what one has learned in order to capture the spirit of ethical prescriptions rather than unthinkingly following instructions. The inevitability of conflicts and uncertainties in ethics means that one must learn not just what to do in this or that particular case and not just some guidelines or principles, but one needs a set of priorities and a way of thinking about them.

The most common conflicts are those between one's own self-interest and dictates of morality. On the one hand, you really want to do something; on the other hand, it is immoral. Or, on the one side, you see a clear path to fulfilling a life-long ambition; on the other, you would have to lie, cheat, steal, or betray a friend in order to take that path. Doing the right thing does not always or even usually involve acting against your own best interests, but it sometimes does, such as when you now find that keeping that promise you made some time ago has become extremely inconvenient or expensive. Indeed, even when one's self-interest clearly coincides with what one ought to do, we often make a distinction between doing what one ought to do *because* it is the right thing to do and doing it just because what is right happens to be in one's self-interest. Thus it is important to distinguish the morally right thing to do from what is simply prudent. But then again, the moral skeptic might well ask why one should ever act contrary to his or her own self-interests—unless, of course, doing so (in the short run) will serve one's longer-term interests. If the aim and justification of morality were just to serve our ultimate self-interests, then such cases as the above would suggest—what is intolerable—that it is all right to be immoral if it is in one's better interests.

The question "What is morality and how is it justified?" has become one of the leading questions of ethics. In the introduction, we pointed out that morality and moral rules were distinguished by their importance and priority, by their universality, rationality and objectivity, and by their unselfish concern for others. But even within these guidelines (which are themselves often a matter of some dispute, as we shall see) there is ample room for alternative interpretations and justifications for what is meant by "morality." In this chapter, we shall see that there are quite a few distinctive theories of morality, all of them in at least partial conflict with each other and none of them entirely adequate by itself. Some are concerned primarily to explain the *authority* of morality, that is, the power or right of morality to command our obedience, even when its dictates are contrary to our interests. Others are concerned primarily to make the connection with self-interest, personal happiness, and the public good. Some are concerned primarily to emphasize the special rational and objective status of morality, while others are out to reduce morality to less honorable motives and undermine its special importance. Indeed, whether all of these theories deserve to be called *theories of morality* is itself an essential part of the debate, for the reasons we discussed in Chapter 1. Does morality require obedience, and if so, to what or to whom? Is morality compatible with self-interest and/or the public good? Under what conditions and in what circumstances? What does it mean to say that morality or moral rules are objective? And is there any special domain of human behavior and concern that deserves to be called moral, as opposed to a more general concern for personal integrity and the public good?

DOING THE RIGHT THING:
THE EXAMPLE OF SOCRATES

If you were to face an ultimate conflict between obedience to morality and your own happiness, what would you choose? Suppose there were no question but that the moral choice would preclude any further happiness, if, for instance, the decision were one which could cost you your life. There may be no situation that provides a keener sense and a more indisputable test of one's ultimate values than such a truly life-or-death decision. One is forced to choose; morality—or one's life.

In the history of philosophy, there has been no more dramatic presentation of this ultimate moral test than the case of Socrates, the great Greek philosopher who was condemned to death in ancient Athens. In 399 BC, Socrates was already an old man over seventy, but he had made a considerable reputation (and a nuisance) of himself by challenging the favorite assumptions of the leading politicians of the city. He also made many enemies and, finally, he was accused of "corrupting the minds" of the young students who flocked around him. After a lengthy and famous trial, he was sentenced to die by drinking hemlock, a deadly poison that causes great pain and violent convulsions before taking its final, fatal effect. In his trial (reported to us in Plato's dialogue, *Apology*), Socrates defends philosophy and attacks the unsound opinions of the *hoi polloi*—the mass of ordinary citizens. He maintains his innocence and argues that the charge is unjust. He even suggests to the jury that he should receive a pension instead of punishment. But despite his eloquence, the jury goes against him, and Socrates is sent off to prison to await his execution.

In prison, however, Socrates has the opportunity to escape. His friend Crito comes to him and reports that Socrates's many friends and admirers have already lined up a number of crucial bribes and escape routes as well as a safe haven for Socrates in exile. His family and friends will be with him and, still in exceptional health, he will be able to look forward to at least several more years of happiness. But Socrates, in Plato's dialogue *Crito,* produces an argument that has been immensely unsettling to philosophers and philosophy students ever since. The pursuit of happiness and the injustice of the sentence are not enough to justify his escaping, he argues with Crito, who becomes increasingly upset with his seemingly stubborn teacher. *Reason* tells him that what he *ought* to do is to stay and be executed; his personal pleasures are not ultimately important, he insists. The injustice of the sentence and the abuse of the law are not grounds for disobeying and rejecting the law itself. One can defy authorities (as Socrates often did), but one is still bound by reason and law.

Socrates's argument begins by insisting that personal considerations—one's emotions and desires—must not determine one's course of action. Reason must do that. Furthermore, Socrates several times rejects Crito's argument that virtually *everyone* thinks that Socrates would be right to escape. "We should not care what people in general think," he insists. The only consideration is what is *right,* and reason alone will tell us this. And what is right, Socrates goes on to argue, is to act for the good of one's "soul." This means, he argues, to obey the laws of the state even when they are unjust. Not to do so would be to betray oneself, as well as to weaken the power of the laws by making oneself an exception (and thereby encouraging others to do so too). By remaining in Athens, Socrates continues, he has agreed, in effect, to obey its laws, and now he has an *obligation* to continue to do so, even when those laws turn against him. It is doing good itself that is his ultimate concern. Nevertheless, Socrates concludes, in respecting the law he is also doing what is best for himself and everyone else. The best way to live is to always do the right thing, even if doing the right thing undermines the pleasures of life or—life itself.

Socrates knew that he had done right and had been treated unfairly by the court. He then faced an unenviable choice: to turn down the offer to escape and face death or to leave Athens for sanctuary elsewhere and live the rest of his life with the knowledge that he had violated his trust and done wrong. He chose to stay and be executed on the ground that there are matters more important than even life itself. That which is most worth living for may also be worth dying for.

If you had been in Socrates's position, what would you have done? If you decided to escape, how would you defend your decision against someone who accused you of violating your own moral principles by flouting the law? What are the implications of your answer?

MORALITY AND THE LAW:
THE PROBLEM OF AUTHORITY

Socrates's decision to face execution rather than to escape and continue his happy life made him the most celebrated philosophical hero of all times and a champion of the moral life. But the motivation behind Socrates's decision was by no means obvious, nor indeed was the nature of the decision itself. On the one hand, he clearly argues that one has an obligation to obey the law of the land and accept the authority of the state, even where the result is injustice. But, on the other hand, it is not as if obeying the law of the land as such was Socrates's highest priority, and it was not for the sake of the laws of Athens that he died. In the *Apology,* he argues quite emphatically (as

Jesus and his followers would argue several centuries later) that the Good is above the law and that there are circumstances in which one should conscientiously break the law, as Socrates did when he insisted on continuing to teach philosophy despite the official warnings against his doing so. And even in the *Crito,* he quite explicitly argues that it is for his own sake, for the sake of his soul, that he is sacrificing his life, not just for the sake of the laws of Athens, with which he often disagreed. But then, what is the relationship between—that is, the laws of particular societies—and morality? Should we obey the laws only when we find reason to do so but break laws when we disagree with them? Where does our obligation to obey the law come from? Obeying the law in general, would seem to be a moral obligation if anything is. But what gives the laws their authority, and what gives morality its ultimate authority?

If morality is to be something more than mere prudence or the projection of our own personal prejudices onto others, it must have *authority.* Authority is, first of all, a kind of power, legitimate power, which overrides personal interests and preferences and provides a source of appeal for disputes and disagreements. Socrates, by virtue of his wisdom and (in retrospect) his heroic status, had enormous moral authority. But Socrates continuously complained about his personal "ignorance" and always appealed to "higher" laws, ultimately to the Good itself, to justify his actions and opinions. Indeed, his appeal to the law in *Crito* is just one of many such appeals to higher authority, and his decision to obey the law—even where the law was wrong— was just one more way of emphasizing the relative unimportance of one person's life compared to the Good as such. It is the Good itself, the ultimate ideal that informs everything that we do, that gives authority to all particular acts and decisions as well as to the particular laws of a particular state or society. Good laws are such only insofar as they conform to this ultimate authority.

But what is this ultimate authority, and how does one recognize it? Is there an ultimate ideal that informs everything and everyone everywhere? Many philosophers and a great many jurists and lawyers have backed away from this difficult philosophical question and have attempted instead to rest the case for morality on the local laws of the land. There, at least, we have something explicit, written in black and white, before us, and while we might debate at length about the cor- rect interpretation of a law or whether a law ought to be repealed, at least we know that it *is* the law and where its authority lies. Its author- ity lies in the state and in the society as a whole. But is this enough?

Some philosophers would argue that what is right is defined and determined by the law, and whatever the law says is obligatory—whether or not there are good reasons for changing the law. But where would these reasons come from, and aren't there considerations outside of the law that weigh on our sense of obligation as heavily as the authority of the law?

The thesis that what is right is defined and determined by the law would seem to follow from our strong emphasis on the importance of ethos in ethics, for it is the culture as a whole that determines both its own morals and its legal system. This move also tends to satisfy many relativists, who would insist that there is nothing outside of a culture to which its morals can be appealed. But this is a troubling conclusion, for example, when a society commits what seem to us to be the most foul crimes against its own citizens. And there are serious problems with this attempt to reduce morality and the Good to a particular society's laws. The law of the land makes claims only upon the inhabitants (and visitors) to that land, but morality claims to be universal and apply everywhere. The laws of a land may be immoral, and there are corrupt, unjust legal systems. There are bad and even evil societies. (Nazi Germany and *apartheid* South Africa are the two most frequent examples.) Furthermore, it is clear that not all citizens of a country agree on many moral matters, whether or not they agree about the laws which give the society its guidelines. One of the enduring disputes in the philosophy of law is precisely the question whether one can or should legislate morals, and the very question makes it evident that the power and sanctions of the law of the land are one thing and morals another. Moreover, when one considers the origins of laws—whether in the pronouncements of a dictator, passed by popular legislation by a democratic majority or as handed down through the ages by tradition—it is clear that there are no guarantees that laws will always be good and several reasons to suppose that, at least sometimes, they might not be. As society changes, laws become out of date. The politics of the moment sometimes overwhelms good moral sense and the law becomes a tangle of impossible demands. A society's legal system and its rules of ethics, including its moral rules, are not the same.

Part of what makes Socrates's arguments and decision so difficult is that in his case, the judgment of law is so clearly unfair, even, we might say, immoral. It would seem plausible to argue that it is, *in general,* morally right to obey the law—indeed, one might insist that one *always* has an obligation to obey the law *except when there is an overwhelming reason not to.* But this qualification, even if it applies only rarely, is extremely important. What will *not* count as an "overwhelming reason," of course, will be mere strong personal interest; one is not justified in cheating on the federal income tax (which would be breaking the law) merely on the ground that one really needs the money to buy a new sailboat. But one might well have an overwhelming reason to break a particular law if that law seems to contradict some "higher" principle of morality. Thus, pacifists may refuse to pay their taxes on the ground that taxes are used to fight wars which they consider immoral, and some go to prison rather than fight in a war which they consider to be immoral.

The *Crito* does not give us a clear way of understanding conflicts between morality and the law, but Plato's view of the Good does provide us with an excellent if obscure way of understanding this conflict. The Good, like God, stands above all laws and man-made customs; it therefore provides an absolute standard by which all local laws can be evaluated. For example, many states once had laws allowing slavery and denying even the most basic economic rights to women and children. But the Good, one might argue, includes the demand that all people have rights, including the right to certain minimal freedoms which slavery denies. (It is worth noting, however, that Plato lived in a society that accepted slavery as "natural.") Where the law violates our conception of the Good, many good citizens are willing to argue that the moral thing to do is to break the law—while also trying to change them. There are moral ideals and authority above the law of the land, and "the Good" is convenient shorthand for making this point. But what, then, is the Good?

THE GOOD AND GOD'S WILL

The one fact which almost everyone agrees would have profound authority in moral matters and would justify morality beyond question is the existence of an all-knowing, all-powerful, just and beneficent God. One need not say that the words *good* and *ought mean* "commanded by God," but it is clear that the notion of the Good would be clarified and the quest for justification would be solved if we could know that certain things are good and right *because* God commands them, whether or not the fact of God's existence logically entails the goodness of His commands.

One problem is that we don't seem to know, with any certainty or singularity, exactly what it is that God commands. The Bible is not a document written in a single voice. The Old and New Testaments depict God and His behavior quite differently and, consequently, they offer us different conceptions of morality. Even within the Old and New Testaments there are a number of different viewpoints and, with them, somewhat different views of morality. At the risk of gross over-simplification, we might mention, for example, that the God of the Old Testament is sometimes introduced as a "jealous," and at times "wrathful," God who nevertheless watches over His "chosen people" and assures them victory in battle. Elsewhere in the Old Testament, God tests His people, allows their temples and their homeland to be destroyed and sometimes (as in the story of Job) subjects His people to excruciating torments. The God of the New Testament is celebrated rather as a "loving" God who is not so concerned with punishing us as with "saving" us through His own sacrifice. Even the Gospels give us significantly different portraits of Christ, which have given rise to very different interpretations of the meaning of God and Christianity as a whole.

The ethical visions that emerge from these conceptions of God differ accordingly: the Old Testament places its emphasis on obedience and God's Law. The New Testament, rather, takes as its highest commandment that we should *love* one another, which may be quite different from dutifully obeying the Law. It would be a mistake to suggest that these ethical views are incompatible (one can be loving and obedient at the same time), but it would also be a mistake to ignore the differences. Morality, as defined by God in the Bible, is not a singular set of commandments.

Nevertheless, it may be argued, there is sufficient agreement on the main matters of morality. There may be disagreements about the moral status of opening shops on the Sabbath and working mothers, but there is no disagreement about the prohibitions on murder, stealing, and adultery. There may be difficulties in using the Bible to answer day-to-day questions about our behavior, but there is no question about the fact that the Bible provides us with a general conception and justification of morality. Whether or not there are problems with particular applications of some universal commandments, the general nature of Judeo-Christian morality seems sufficiently clear.

Many people attempt to bypass problems of Biblical interpretation by appealing directly to the presence of God within, a feeling of God "in one's heart" or, more accurately, in terms of personal faith and individual conscience. One need not doubt or belittle the importance of such religious feelings and promptings in order to question their dependability as a source of moral directives and justification. How does one know that the promptings of one's "heart" or conscience are indeed the Will of God? History is full of insane people who have felt such promptings acutely and had no doubts about their divine origin. Most likely, we know that the promptings of our heart or conscience are good because they conform to the morality taught in the Bible. Thus we do not interpret the occasional urge to kill as a divine message, but we do so interpret the quiet urge to forgive someone.

Even if one ignores questions of interpretation and accepts without question the idea that the Bible is the literal, revealed word of God, there are difficult questions confronting the most faithful reader. There are certain commandments and descriptions of the acts of God in the Bible—for example, God's order to Abraham to kill his son and His treatment of Job—which demand a justification. Family murder and wanton cruelty to the innocent are actions which we find morally intolerable. God on occasion wipes out entire populations by fire and/or flood, presumably including a number of innocent children. And even apart from these acts of Biblical vengeance, we can think of hundreds of "acts of God"—hurricanes, floods, and earthquakes—in which the innocent have perished. What are we to make of this as ethics? Are God's actions and commands always moral?

Three answers have been most prevalent in the long history of this discussion.

- The first answer is that if God did or commanded these things, *therefore* they are good, without any qualification.

- The second answer is that these things, which seem to us to be very evil, are in fact good after all. (An appeal to "God's mysterious ways" or G. W. Leibniz's famous suggestion that this is, despite its problems, "the best of all possible worlds.")

- Third, one can acknowledge that these acts are immoral and conclude that not everything that God does or commands is good.

(There is a fourth answer, of course, which is to insist that there is no God or, that even if there were a God, He would make no difference to morality. We will not consider this reply here, since it obviously eliminates the question.)

The first answer is the straightforward acceptance of the thesis that God's will *defines* the Good, and if God does something out of line with what we call "morality," what He does is, nevertheless, good. This raises a problem, however, for, if one accepts these biblical accounts, one will conclude that God does not always insist on what we call "morality." Of course, we can and do revise our sense of morality to accord with our interpretation of the Bible and our experience, so this should be seen as a dynamic interpretive process, not just a matter of simple agreement or disagreement. Nevertheless, we may be uncomfortable with the idea that whatever God does or directs is therefore good, for this makes it impossible to even raise the question whether God would or could do wrong.

The second answer allows one to keep both the view that what God wills is good and the thesis that God justifies morality. That is its perennial appeal. The problem raised by the second answer is how to argue that God's sometimes brutal biblical behavior can be understood as moral nevertheless. By appealing to "mysterious ways," one might save faith but thereby lose the direct and obvious connection between God and morality. To say that something is a mystery is not to explain or understand it; it is, instead, to insist that one cannot explain or understand it. We seem to require some independent conception of morality, such that we can then go on to show or believe that God's will is in accordance with it.

The third and last answer accepts the conclusion that there is a difference between God, God's will, and morality, but this means, in effect, we give up the idea that God alone can justify morality. We must have some independent conception and justification of morality, which may or may not apply to God as well. The third answer openly entails this view, where the second seems, rather, to be forced into it. Of course, almost anyone who believes in the traditional Judeo-Christian God will also believe that God does in fact only good. But to believe that he does so *in fact* and not by definition is an importance difference. One wants to believe that God is good, but it hardly serves as a proof to simply define whatever God does as good.

The conclusion that we have to know what is good apart from our belief in God goes back as far as Plato. In a dialogue called the *Euthyphro,* he considers the question whether something is good or right because God (the gods) commands it, or whether God (the gods) commands it because it is good or right. Socrates quickly convinces Euthyphro of the latter position, which means that what is good is good apart from the fact that God (the gods) wills it. Even if one is not troubled by the examples in the Bible, one can consider the following thought experiment. Suppose someone were to uncover what seemed to be an authentic original manuscript from the Bible which gave us a perverse set of commandments, such as "Thou shalt kill," "Thou shalt steal," and "Thou shalt commit adultery as much as thou wouldst." Would we not reject the manuscript, its apparent authenticity aside, just because of our conviction that God would not command such immorality? But that means that we have a conception of morality which does not depend wholly on God's will; to the contrary, we are confident that God wills us to be moral because we believe that God Himself is a moral being.

The idea that God is the authority upon which morality is based need not mean that morality is justified because God wills it, however. It has often been suggested that God justifies morality because He *sanctions* it, that is, He sees to it that those who are moral are (eventually) rewarded and that those who are evil are (eventually) punished. This assurance is perfectly compatible with the idea that morality is quite independent of God's will. This view of God as sanction provides an excellent reason for being moral, namely, that one ought to be moral if one wants to avoid a dreadful punishment, and possibly gain a considerable reward as well.

The problem with this familiar viewpoint is that it confuses a purely selfish *motive* for being moral with the *justification* of morality. It makes morality a matter of *prudence,* which is precisely what the appeal to God as the justification of morality is intended to avoid. If morality is justified by appeal to God, it is because morality thereby becomes something more than an appeal to our own self-interests, namely, obedience to and love of an all-powerful, all-knowing, just and beneficent Being. To confuse the prudential advantages of believing in God and being moral with the justification of morality by appeal to God's goodness is to undermine precisely this reason for turning to God in the first place. God's will defines morality not because what he commands is in our interests, but because God is the ultimate moral *authority.*

One final point about God and the Good. There is at least one crucial virtue in Christian theology that is sometimes elevated "above morality," and that is the virtue of *faith.* So long as faith is one of the cardinal virtues and is understood (as Kant, for example, understood it) as directed toward morality, there is no difficulty. But if faith in God is set apart and put "above" morality, belief in God may not serve as a justification of morality at all. The Danish philosopher Kierkegaard, for example, argues that this is the point of the Abraham and Isaac story in Genesis. Because he must prove his faith in God by committing the most immoral of acts, Abraham is forced to choose between faith and morality. The fact that God stops the sacrifice and gives the story a "happy ending" does not alter the fact that faith and morality can be opposed as well as conjoined.

TELEOLOGY AND HUMAN NATURE

A nontheological way to introduce the notion of authority into ethics is by an appeal to nature, for example, pointing out the fact that something serves a certain natural purpose. Thus one can say that the value of the heart in an animal is the fact that its purpose is to pump the blood around the body. This raises a further question, "What is the purpose of pumping the blood around the body?" But this too can be answered in terms of a purpose (to carry food and oxygen to the body, eliminate waste, etc.). Eventually, we will reach an answer citing the purpose, "to keep the creature alive," at which point we may want to know whether there is some purpose to this. A practical if not very sentimental answer might be, "Yes, we need pork from the pig as food in the fall." A more philosophical answer might be, "Because every living thing has its place in nature." But, especially when the creature in question is one of us, we demand a sense of some further purpose, built into human nature, which, in addition to making life worth living, may also provide a justification for morality.

The philosophical term for such purposive explanations and justifications is *teleology*. The word comes from the Greek word for purpose, *telos*. Aristotle, most famously, gives a *teleological* justification of moral virtue in his *Nicomachean Ethics*. He argues the teleological position explicitly in the well-known opening sentence of that work: "Every art and every kind of inquiry, and likewise every act and purpose, seems to aim at some good; and so it has been well said that the good is that at which everything aims." In the case of human action, Aristotle argues, this ultimate good is "happiness" (*eudaimonia*), the life of virtuous action in accordance with reason. How does he come to this conclusion? It is essential to human nature, he argues, to be rational. Our purpose in life, therefore, is to be as rational as possible, and being so is, if successful, happiness. Thus morality may be nothing less than obedience to our own natures, revealed to us as the moral authority of reason.

A teleological justification of morality appeals to some overriding goal, built into human nature or nature in general. We have mentioned that Aristotle takes this ultimate goal to be happiness, but we have not yet said that this goal is part of a much larger scheme of things in which Aristotle speculates upon the purpose of human existence and, ultimately, the purpose of the existence of the world. A teleological justification of morality, in other words, is a demonstration that our moral principles and virtues fit into some larger purpose. In the preceding section, we considered the possibility that our purpose in life might be a divine purpose, an expression of God's will. Jean-Paul Sartre's response to this might be worth noting. He insists that if there is no God, there is no divine "design" that gives meaning to our lives. Expressing a similar view, the Russian novelist Fyodor Dostoevsky has one of his characters (Ivan Karamazov) declare, "If there is no God, everything is permitted." But the purpose of life does not have to come from God, and if there is a God, as we have seen, it does not follow that what is good is determined by Him. Indeed, there is good reason to reject that view. Aristotle does not appeal to God in his theory of the "function," or *telos,* of human life, and one can appeal to "nature's purpose" in support of human morality with or without reference to any divine purpose. For example, some contemporary anthropologists and sociobiologists have suggested that we are by nature a cooperative species with built-in social instincts, a view propounded by Aristotle almost twenty-five hundred years ago when he defined human beings as "social animals."

Finally, in addition to God's purpose and nature's purpose, there are *our* purposes. If we could show, for example, that all human behavior is aimed at a single end, then that end might in turn serve as the justification of morality. Aristotle's suggestion that happiness is such an end has been repeated many times by many philosophers, throughout history. Another prominent candidate has been pleasure, and the *hedonist's* thesis that all our actions ultimately aim at maximizing pleasure and minimizing pain might also serve as a justification of morality, assuming, that is, that one can show that morality does indeed lead to maximum pleasure and minimum pain. So, too, people have often argued (particularly in times of turmoil) that the ultimate purpose of human life is to live and prosper together in harmony. Our ultimate *telos* is thus truly a social purpose rather than a set of individual goals.

A different kind of candidate for our ultimate purpose in life, which Aristotle conjoins with happiness, is reason. But reason as our *telos* raises certain difficult questions, since reason also provides the primary basis for a very different set of theories about morality, namely, *deontological* theories. Immanuel Kant, for example, offers a teleological argument (much like Aristotle's) to the effect that reason is our ultimate purpose in life and therefore we ought to be rational. But Kant then becomes the paragon deontologist and goes on to argue that morality is to be justified by appeal to reason itself, *not* by appeal to our purposes in life (our "inclinations," such as the desire to be happy). Nevertheless, it is essential to Kant's entire philosophy that reason is our ultimate purpose in life as well as the basis of morality. (Perhaps the warning here is that one should always be wary of broad philosophical categories; the great philosophers almost always transcend them.)

Aristotle's teleological approach to ethics appeals only to human nature. It does not refer human nature to God. But after Aristotle, much of Christian ethics adopted his idea that that morality was a function of human reason and developed this idea in *Natural Law Theory*. According to the Theory of Natural Law, human rationality has been created in us by God and in the image of God, who himself is the perfectly rational being. Saint Thomas Aquinas, the greatest of the Natural Law theorists, equated the moral life with the life of reason, stamped in us by God, and insisted that to attack reason was equivalent to condemning God. But the difference between Natural Law Theory and the idea that the dictates of morality are defined by God's will is all-important here. According to the view that the dictates of morality are defined by God's will, morality could have been otherwise, in fact, anything God might command, however unreasonable. Nor is there any assurance on that view that we are rational creatures, capable of ascertaining what is right or wrong ourselves. But Natural Law Theory does provide such assurances and, furthermore, maintains the argument that we know the good and the right through reason, not by way of commandments from God, even if it is also true that God gave us the rational capacity to do so. It also means that belief in God is not a prerequisite for being moral, since God made believers and nonbelievers alike rational and capable of moral judgment, Believers realize that their reason is a gift of God, a "divine spark" within them; nonbelievers do not. They may disagree on matters of religion, but, according to Natural Law Theory, they share the same God-given rational human nature and, accordingly, the same concept of morality.

What about *our* purposes? Is there a single ultimate purpose to all our lives? Or, even if there is not a single purpose that is part of human nature as such, can we not justify morality by appeal to the various purposes we pursue in life? We can do so as long as we are willing to be explicit about the *hypothetical* nature of such justifications. For example, if we want to be respected in our own communities, we might well defend the hypothetical imperative, "If you want to be respected, then be moral and virtuous." Indeed, most of our desires in life—which are not only conducted but made possible and meaningful in society—lend themselves to such hypothetical imperatives. One might accordingly argue that morality is a system of hypothetical imperatives, each of them conditional on some purpose or other that people pursue. Does this mean that all possible purposes require morality, that there is nothing that people might want which is better obtained by being immoral rather than moral? No, there will always be some people with purposes that dictate immorality. But they are far fewer than moral cynics have sometimes suggested, and, furthermore, it will be necessary for *our* purposes to thwart such people and their purposes. Such a qualified teleological view may therefore not provide the universal and absolute justification of morality sought by some philosophers, but it does supply a modest justification for most people. We can best get what we want out of life by being moral and virtuous. But this need not imply that morality is just a *means* to happiness. It may also be, as Aristotle insists, an essential *part* of happiness. In other words, one of our purposes in life is to be a "good person." This goal already has morality built into it, not just as a means but as an end. It could then be the *telos* of what we consider best in ourselves.

ENLIGHTENED EGOISM

The suggestion that morality can be justified by showing that it is conducive to our purposes marks a shift away from a more impersonal justification of morality by appeal to some outside authority, such as God or human nature in general, and toward a more personally oriented justification in terms of our aims and interests. One aspect of this shift is that it places the burden of justification on the ability of morality to satisfy our individual interests. The grounding or justification of morality, then, lies not in some higher good or authority but in its effectiveness in helping us to live well. But do morality and self-interest go hand in hand? Surely this is not always the case, for the dictates of morality sometimes directly contradict our immediate interests. Accordingly, the essential task of this kind of theory, which typically goes by the name *enlightened egoism,* is to formulate a plausible hypothesis concerning the relationship between morality and self-interest. There are numerous variations.

1. *Acting morally will always lead to the satisfaction of one's own interests.* This assumption would make life a lot easier, if it were true; we would never have to choose between what we want to do and what we ought to do. Unfortunately, the thesis is not very plausible, and life is accordingly not so simple.

2. *Acting morally will usually lead to the satisfaction of one's own interests.* This thesis is certainly more plausible, and insofar as many of our interests include moral ambitions and are perfectly compatible with morality, it is safe enough. It does not do, however, what the enlightened egoist wants it to do: show that one is justified in pursuing one's own self-interest—even in those cases in which morality and self-interest seem to conflict.

3. *Acting morally will usually, in the long run, lead to the satisfaction of more of one's interests than would be satisfied if one did not act morally.* Not surprisingly, the more one weakens the enlightened egoist's thesis, the more plausible it becomes. Nevertheless, this point would still be a hard one to prove to a very clever villain.

4. *Acting morally will, overall, serve the greatest number of interests of the greatest number of people, including oneself.* We are now, however, beyond the range of egoism—enlightened or otherwise. It is one thing to claim that acting morally serves one's *own* interests; it is quite different to claim that acting morally serves a number of interests, including the interests of other people. This is no longer an egoistic position. It is called "utilitarianism," and we will examine it in the following section.

5. *Acting morally will, in addition to helping to satisfy some of one's own interests, set an example which will make the world a better place in which to live.* Thus it may satisfy other interests that have not been considered or have been given up as hopeless, such as encouraging friendliness in the streets, making everyone more cooperative and dependable and making life generally more enjoyable.

This version, unlike the others, is both egoist and edifying. It still appeals to one's own self interest, but in such a way that it obviously has appeal to most people's shared interests and concerns as well. Moreover, the causal thesis suggested here is probably true. The world would very likely be a more satisfying place if everyone were moral and virtuous. Unfortunately, many people would have to see this happen *before* they agreed to cooperate, and some people would inevitably find that, in a trusting, benign world, the profits of immorality would be even higher and the risks considerably lower. Such has been the undoing of many a pleasant society.

6. *Acting morally, whether or not it results in the satisfaction of one's own interest, inspires feelings of self-righteousness and well-being which are their own satisfactions.* In other words, goodness is its own reward. No doubt this is often true, but what if other rewards are more attractive? Does feeling righteous alone suffice to make a person moral, or is it, at best, one more motive—among many others—which makes being moral more attractive? It is a matter of common experience that self-righteousness can be extremely satisfying. But it is also a matter of common experience that many people find certain immoral satisfactions far more attractive.

There are other formulations, but these will do as representatives of the position which is sometimes called enlightened egoism. It is egoism insofar as the focus of one's concern and the sole ground of justification is the appeal to one's own interests. It is enlightened insofar as it is not merely selfish but open to the suggestion that acting morally may serve one's own interests better. The problem with all such justifications, however, is that they tend to lose hold of the aim of a moral theory, which is to justify morality in terms of some authority *apart* from our purely personal interests. In other words, they tend, at best, to be prudential guidelines rather than justifications of morality as such. Morality, it is usually argued, always extends beyond the individual and his or her interests. The justification of morality, therefore, must go beyond personal interests too. What is even worse, however, is that such theories, even as prudential guidelines, tend to fail just when they are needed most—for example, when the reward for wrong-doing is huge and the threat of getting caught very small. One might well talk a petty thief out of a small sum by raising the prospect of going to prison, but one will hardly so influence the mobster who knows the enormous size of the stakes and the very remote chance of being caught and convicted.

MORAL SENTIMENT THEORY

The most direct opponent of egoism in all its forms—whether psychological or ethical, whether crude or enlightened—is moral sentiment theory. Moral sentiment theory, in a word, is the theory that we are "naturally" motivated by unselfish concerns, including what David Hume and Adam Smith called *sympathy*. They attacked the earlier "selfishness" theories of Hobbes and argued that in addition to self-interest we are endowed by nature with such considerate emotions as justice, benevolence, compassion, and pity. Jean-Jacques Rousseau eloquently argued a

Continental version of moral sentiment theory. They all agreed that self-interest was not the only effective motive, and that morality consisted at least in part of our natural concern for other people. On some of the fine points, there was disagreement. Smith thought justice (that is, not wanting to harm others) was natural while Hume thought that it was "artificial" (in other words, cultivated and learned in society). Hume changed his mind about the relationship between benevolence and sympathy and Rousseau shied away from sympathy and rather spoke of our "indifference" to others. Furthermore, what Hume and Smith meant by sympathy was what we, today, would call *empathy*, the ability to (in some sense) share the feelings of others, in particular, to feel pained because they are in pain. Thus it is more than "to feel sorry for."

If sympathy (literally, "feeling with") is the sharing of feeling, or, as a disposition, the ability to share the feelings of others, it includes sharing their joys and anger, as well as their suffering. One need not "agree with" in the sense of "approve of" the feeling in question, of course, any more than must always enjoy, like, or approve of one's own emotions. The feelings may agree but we need not; sharing a feeling is one thing but accepting or approving of the feeling something quite different. In a bad movie, we might share the offended hero's sense of revenge while berating ourselves for just that feeling. We might find ourselves sympathizing with someone envious or hateful and nevertheless criticize ourselves for doing so, thus sharing but not at all accepting or approving of the envy or the hatred.

Sympathy so conceived is thus not actually a sentiment at all but rather a *vehicle* for understanding other people's sentiments, "a fellow-feeling with any passion whatever."[1] Smith goes on to qualify this by insisting that sympathy is *not* an actual sharing of sentiments (in the sense of "having the same feeling"). It is rather an act of imagination by which one can appreciate the feelings of another person by "putting oneself in his place." This provides both Hume and Smith with a way of accounting for how it can be that people are not essentially selfish or self-interested but are essentially social creatures who can act on behalf of others whose feelings they do not literally share. But moral sentiment theory also makes the serious claim that sympathy motivates moral behavior. (Hume famously says that "reason is and ought to be slave of the passions.") We will see that this claim about motivation is the most dramatic difference between Kant and the Scots, namely, whether practical reason can itself be motivating. (Kant thinks so. Hume thinks not.)

---

1 *Theory of the Moral Sentiments* I.i.5.

Hume and Smith celebrate sympathy as a "natural" emotion or sentiment and as the basis for all morality, although their notion of "sympathy" is both ambiguous (between sympathy, empathy, and benevolence, for instance) and over-ambitious (it is sometimes called upon to do *all* of the moral work). Sympathy is often equated with compassion and the root meanings are, to be sure, the same ("feeling with"), but the two terms have a very different connotation. Sympathy is sometimes equated with care, in the obvious sense that to sympathize with someone is to care about him, to see his pain or suffering as *mattering*. But "care" is also multiply ambiguous, for example between caring *about* and caring *for*, the latter implying some sort of behavior, the former not. Moreover, there is pity, but, again, pity carries with it a note of condescension, and while having compassion for someone is usually most welcome, having pity for them is not.

What is it to "share" a feeling, as sympathy (empathy) seems to require? One might well argue that it is a matter of logic that each person can have his and only his own feeling. Two people can share the same *kind* of feeling, indeed, the same kind of feeling about the same object or situation at the same time. For example, there is what contemporary psychologists refer to as "emotional contagion," the fact that people "pick up" the emotions from others nearby. The angry mood of a crowd is an unfortunately familiar example. But so too is the mood in a comedy club. Sympathy (like contemporary empathy) also admits of a range of interpretations, from the highly imaginative (actively imagining oneself in the other person's position) to the minimally imaginative and basically affective (finding oneself extremely uncomfortable in the presence of someone in pain). Hume and Smith shift between these two extremes, but both defend the most imaginative position of adopting the viewpoint of an "impartial spectator" who has removed all self-interest from moral judgment. Again, the idea is that morality and human behavior in general need not be motivated by self-interest, and the undeniable truth of moral sentiment theory is that we are essentially and "naturally" social creatures with fellow-feeling, care and sympathy for others.

UTILITARIANISM

The most influential theory of morality of the past century or so has been the theory called *utilitarianism*. It is at once a metaethical theory concerning the justification of morality and a formulation of the *summum bonum*—a single principle which will tell us how we ought to act.

61

It is distinctively a teleological theory, emphasizing pleasure or happiness as the desired and desirable end of all human action. Morality is a means—and its principles act as "rules of thumb"—to maximize happiness all around. The classic formulation of utilitarianism, accordingly, is to act so as to produce "the greatest good for the greatest number." This is what John Stuart Mill calls "the utility principle." It is a theory that insists on disinterestednss as well as self-interest, insofar as we must consider everyone's happiness, and not just our own. It is a theory about what is rational as well as what is right; it tells us both how to be happy and what we ought to do. What is not clear is the extent to which it is a distinctive theory of *morality,* for what might be good for the greatest number may nevertheless turn out to be immoral, and what is obviously moral may turn out not to maximize happiness.

Utilitarianism begins with the view that what motivates us is first our own happiness, but it then derives the general objective principle that we ought therefore to act not just for our own happiness but for "the greatest good for the greatest number." It is a theory which tends to put much more emphasis on results than on principles and intentions, however. Obedience to the utility principle is not nearly so essential to the evaluation of actions and particular rules as the *consequences* of those actions and rules. This has misled many people to define utilitarianism as any ethical theory that worries only about consequences (a set of theories much better called *consequentialism*), but this focus is not its defining characteristic. Utilitarianism is essentially a teleological theory which emphasizes pleasure or happiness as the ultimate end of action. It is not at all blind or indifferent to intentions or rules, but the emphasis is on beneficial and harmful results rather than on a "good will" alone, which, however well-intended, may nonetheless make everyone miserable.

Utilitarianism, in one sense, goes back to the beginning of ethics (thus prompting Mill to proclaim that it has been presupposed by every moral philosopher). In the very broad sense that Mill has in mind, utilitarianism is no more than the generally acceptable and minimal view that morality requires that other people's interests must be taken into account, and everyone has an interest in being happy. But, in its more specific versions, utilitarianism is an ethical theory that promises an unusually precise means of calculating what is right and wrong. That promise is, indeed, one of the theory's main attractions. Utilitarianism, properly formulated, will not only show us how morality is to be justified; it will also show us, in detail, exactly what morality is, and what, in every circumstance, we ought to do. The notion of utility presumes that there are discrete quantities of pleasure and pain, which can be measured and compared. We must add to this the second basic principle of utilitarianism, a principle of equality which requires that "each person counts for one and no more than one." In other words, everyone's pleasure (and pain) is to count equally, and it is the overall estimation of pleasure (and pain) that determines what one ought to do.

Utilitarianism had its origins in the Enlightenment, but the founder of the utilitarian movement proper was an English reformer named Jeremy Bentham, who developed a "happiness calculus" to evaluate every action. For every decision, one would add up all the various pleasures it might bring to everyone concerned and subtract the amount of pain. One would compare that total with the amount resulting from alternative courses of action, and one would choose that course of action which maximized pleasure and minimized pain. Bentham's immediate aim was to reform the hopelessly complex and sometimes cruel English legal system by developing a schedule of punishments which would just outweigh the pleasure of a wrongful act, thus minimizing the amount of pain to the smallest degree necessary to deter crime. But the theory also has general application as an overall ethical theory.

Suppose, for example, your elderly grandparents have asked you to come home for Thanksgiving dinner. Unfortunately, however, you have an extremely important and difficult examination on the following Monday, not to mention that some of your friends, who are staying in town, are planning a great party for that Saturday night. Your parents (who know about the exam but not the party) advise you, unhelpfully, "Do what you think best, dear," but you know that they would like to see you with your grandparents. Now, the standard moral evaluation of this situation would raise such questions as "What is your duty in this case?" or "Do you have an obligation to your grandparents?" Not the utilitarian. The question is, rather, which course of action—going home or staying in town—will maximize happiness? You cannot, of course, count your own happiness as more important than that of your parents or grandparents, or, though they are less involved, that of your friends. Your own happiness does count, however, and presumably that will be the first calculation: Which course of action will give you more pleasure and less pain? In the short term, studying is unpleasant (give it a minus 3) but the party will be terrific (plus 6). The trip home is a bit of a hassle (minus 2) but you do like your grandparents (plus 3). You saw your parents two weeks ago, so you don't expect any particular pleasure or pain there, but you do enjoy driving your father's new

63

Grand Prix (plus 2). Longer-term, if you do badly on the exam you may make it hard for yourself for years (minus 12), but if your elderly grandparents should die without your seeing them, you will also feel guilty for years (minus 12). Doing well on the exam will have considerable advantages for the future (plus 12). On the other hand, the feeling of righteousness at having pleased both your parents and your grandparents will be considerable and durable (plus 4). As for your parents, grandparents, and friends, those calculations are rather simple: your grandparents will be delighted to see you (plus 6) and your parents will too (plus 3). If they don't see you, they will be disappointed (minus 3, minus 1). Your friends (you hope) would love you to come to the party (plus 1) but probably won't even notice if you don't (zero). The word "probably," of course, is operative throughout your calculations, and one of the essential ingredients in Bentham's calculus will be the *probability* of each outcome. (For our purpose here, let us assume that all of these probabilities are approximately equal.) Now, according to Bentham, we are in a position to make a completely rational decision without bringing in such obscure and hard to measure concepts as "duty" or "obligation." Our calculation looks like this:

	Go home	Stay and study
	−2	−3
	+3	+6
	+2	−12
	−12	+12
	+4	−3
	+6	−1
	+3	+1
Totals:	+4	0

The answer, clearly, is that you should go home for Thanksgiving.

There are complications not included here, in addition to the obvious difficulties and arbitrariness in quantifying and calculating people's feelings (including one's own). Suppose, though you couldn't have easily predicted such an outcome beforehand, your friends' party got out of hand. The police arrived and arrested several people. (You probably would have been one of them.) That, needless to say, would add considerably to the deficit side of staying in town and going to the party. (In this case, it would not have changed the final outcome.) And you forgot to include in the calculation the fact that you and your father have been having a continuing argument about your buying a car, which might put quite a damper on your rapport with your parents, not only cancelling your Grand Prix driving privileges but making it much less likely that you will get a car of your own (minus 10, cancel plus 2). The probabilities may be small, but they nevertheless complicate the calculation and introduce a new and difficult question: To what extent must the utilitarian calculation take into account all the possible consequences of an action? To the extent we are concerned with the *actual* consequences, it would seem that *all* consequences, no matter how unforeseen or unpredictable, count equally in the calculation of goodness and badness. To the extent that we are concerned just with *envisioned* consequences, on the other hand, we will include only what a responsible person could reasonably expect to happen. One must also add into the calculus the effort, pleasure, and pain that go into the calculation itself. For example, if you spend the two weeks before Thanksgiving worrying about what to do, not studying, and being irritable with your friends and on the phone with your parents, you may well cause yourself and everyone else sufficient pain to cancel out all the expected benefits of the calculations you are trying so rationally to make. Indeed, in many ordinary decisions in life, trying too hard to make a precisely rational decision is itself quite irrational.

Now it may have struck you that this attempt as rational decision-making ultimately seems rather pointless. The numerical amounts of comparative pleasure and pain are difficult to judge and may seem arbitrary. It is not always easy to tell how much you yourself will enjoy yourself or suffer, much less how someone else might enjoy or suffer. But most disturbing of all is the fact that this utilitarian accounting system seems to treat all pleasures and pains on a par, as if there were no difference between them except in their amounts. Bentham himself insisted "Pushpin [a mindless game of the time] is as good as poetry." Thus utilitarianism got an unflattering reputation for being vulgar and without standards.

Accordingly, the ultimate champion of utilitarianism would not be Bentham, but John Stuart Mill, the son of Bentham's colleague, James Mill. Philosophers are famous for their disagreement, and disagreements within agreed-upon viewpoints are often more vehement than disagreements between viewpoints—when theorists often simply refuse to talk to one another. In his definitive pamphlet *Utilitarianism* (1861), Mill defends the principle of utility as the only intelligible basis for ethics, but at the same time he amends Bentham's calculus of sheer *quantity* of pleasure with a conception of the *quality* of pleasure. Thus, "it is better to be a Socrates dissatisfied, than a pig satisfied," Mill writes. This amendment all but destroyed the simplicity of Bentham's calculus, for, after all, it was the apparent ability to calculate all ethical decisions on a single scale of pleasure and pain that made the utilitarian program so appealing to those who wanted straightforward moral solutions. As soon as we add the dimension of quality, that simplicity disappears. It is clear what Mill is concerned about. Suppose one gets much more pleasure in drinking beer than reading Shakespeare. Mill does not want to be forced to conclude that the first act is better than the second. But, once one has shifted the argument away from measurable quantities of pleasure and pain (even assuming that these are available), how does one evaluate their qualities? We have lost our calculus, and it is by no means clear that any more complicated "qualitative" calculus could take its place.

"The greatest good for the greatest number": it sounds like a simple, singular theory. It is not, as we can see from this disagreement between Bentham and Mill on quantity versus quality of pleasure. Indeed, recent theorists have distinguished a surprisingly large number of utilitarian theories, all of them within the "greatest good for the greatest number" idea, but yet significantly different. For example, utilitarianism is sometimes interpreted as a retrospective way of evaluating the actual consequences of actions; sometimes it is interpreted as a technique for planning actions and, accordingly, evaluating intentions rather than consequences, assuming, of course, that good intentions also take into account the probable consequences. Mill himself incorporates both these views, adding that the first is a means of evaluating actions and the second a means of evaluating personal character. Utilitarians are also split on whether or not to accept Mill's and Bentham's too-easy equation of happiness and pleasure. Like Aristotle, many utilitarians want to separate the two and insist that it is happiness that is important, not pleasure as such (though obviously one wouldn't want to suggest that the two are completely opposed). But "happiness," as we have seen, is a broad and equivocal concept, while pleasure and pain at least seem to be precise. Thus more orthodox utilitarians have continued the emphasis on quantifiable (if not qualifiable) pleasure as a way of saving the "utility" of utilitarianism. Other authors have rejected these central ends altogether, preferring to speak only in more noncommittal terms of *preferences*. What remains constant in all versions, of course, is the emphasis on desirable consequences, "the greatest good for the greatest number." But, despite its apparent simplicity, utilitarianism is not a single theory but many, with very different emphases and, appropriately, many different consequences.

Perhaps the most important division among utilitarians today turns on a question we have not yet broached, namely, is it an *individual* action to which we apply the utilitarian calculus, or is it, rather, a *class* of actions? Suppose, for example, I am tempted to tell a lie. This is, of course, one of the standard moral dilemmas, in which the principle of utility is typically thought to be inappropriate. ("It doesn't matter that everyone will be happier if you lie; it's *wrong* to tell a lie!") It is easy to imagine an instance in which the happy consequences of a lie overwhelm the few painful consequences, including the modicum of shame or guilt and the small effort necessary for the cover-up. Furthermore, the consequences of telling the truth would be devastating for the person to whom the upsetting truth is told and, consequently, extremely unpleasant for the truth-teller too. Looking only at this individual act, the utilitarian decision is obvious. One ought to lie, thereby maximizing happiness and minimizing suffering. But, a critic might well contend, it is never an isolated action that is the subject of our deliberations and our ethics. To call an act a "lie" is already to place it in a class of actions which are morally dubious. When we evaluate the consequences of lying, therefore, it is not just a question of whether *this* lie has good or bad consequences for everyone involved. It is a question of whether *lying* as such has good or bad consequences.

This point changes our view of the matter considerably, needless to say. An individual act of lying may well have obviously good consequences, but it is not at all clear that lying *in general* has anything but bad consequences. Lying makes both liars and those lied to unhappy in a myriad of ways, and the "happy" or "white" lie is something of an exception. Thus we can distinguish two distinct forms of utilitarianism (both of which, by the way, seem to be contained in Mill's *Utilitarianism*):

1. Always do that act which will bring the greatest good to the greatest number (*act-utilitarianism*).

2. Always do that *kind* of act (or follow that rule) which will bring the greatest good to the greatest number (*rule-utilitarianism*).

Why have utilitarians split on this seemingly technical issue? (Mill, by contrast, seems content to consider the general implications of an action as part of its consequences; in other words, implicit support for a rule or a class of actions is one of the considerations in deciding the utilitarian "quality" of an act.) The reason is that as act-utilitarianism has been increasingly challenged by difficult cases, rule-utilitarianism has provided a way to save utilitarianism in general from the most troublesome objections. For example, the objection has often been raised that a proper calculation of the consequences of an action is humanly impossible (thus our concern for unforeseen consequences and the difficulty of predicting people's feelings in our Thanksgiving example). But, in rule-utilitarianism, one need not undertake such individual calculations, for they have already been provided in the general form of a rule. Thus, "lying is wrong" is a summary statement of centuries of research and observation: Lying in general leads to bad consequences.

A second much-noted difficulty may be summarized in the following example: Suppose we were to carry out the utilitarian calculations appropriate to two courses of action, one of which includes both a lie and a clearly unfair action in which another person will be cheated. Consider, for example, selling a used car and claiming that it is in excellent running condition, not mentioning that you know that it will fall apart in five miles. Suppose, too, that the balance of utility in your calculation comes out even. Suppose that the person buying the car is quite rich and has several other cars, while you desperately need the money and have to leave town to visit your sickly old uncle. On a strict act-utilitarian basis, the choice between the two is indifferent. Or, if the cheating and lying side emerges a few utility points ahead, you will follow that course of action as the better one.

Not surprisingly, these conclusions are considered to be intolerable by most people. The choice to lie and cheat or not to should never be a matter of indifference, and lying and cheating are not better just because the so-called utility is slightly greater by doing so. One could, as a convinced act-utilitarian, dig in one's heels and insist that such moral concerns are indeed irrelevant and one *should* make decisions only on a strict act-utilitarian basis. But most utilitarians regard such examples as more than sufficient to damage the act-utilitarian theory, and they prefer to modify utilitarianism to get around them. Rule-utilitarianism is the best known of these modifications.

The various forms of utilitarianism—all of them originating in the simple, appealing principle of utility formulated by Bentham and Mill—reflect the problems in the theory. Each variation is an attempt to modify the theory to answer an objection. (The strength and influence of utilitarianism are exemplified by the number of serious revisions of it. Less compelling theories are usually just left to wither away.) The first variation of the theory was Mill's objection to Bentham's purely quantitative theory, which placed too much emphasis on material pleasures and not enough on the harder-to-quantify pleasures of the mind and spirit—the arts, friendship, philosophy. A more recent variation in utilitarian theory is the formulation of rule-utilitarianism—in contrast to act-utilitarianism—as a way of meeting the objection that clearly wrong acts might, in a single instance, be shown to maximize pleasure and minimize pain for everyone involved. Rule-utilitarianism blocks this possibility by insisting that a class of actions, not just a single instance, improves the general well-being. It also accounts for the value of moral rules.

Utilitarianism continues to be one of the most thoroughly discussed ethical theories and strategies of moral justification, but it is not without its continuing problems. As a theory of "utility," it has always been accused of being vulgar and devoid of more spiritual awareness, despite Mill's efforts to add quality to it. Indeed, Mill counters this objection even in *Utilitarianism,* when he answers religious critics who attack him for appealing morality to a business-like calculation of pleasures instead of to God or the Scriptures. Mill's reply is simply that God, being good, wants us to be happy, and so God Himself is a utilitarian and utilitarianism is just a precise way of interpreting God's will.

A more telling set of objections is aimed at the utilitarian emphasis on *consequences* (whether of an action or a class of actions, whether actual consequences or intended consequences). When a moral principle is presented absolutely, as in the Ten Commandments, for example, it is accepted first, and the question of consequences does not arise, or arises only afterward. (Moses did not ask Jehovah, "But what's so bad about people coveting their neighbor's ox?") Such rules may admit of qualifications and exceptions, but their status as rules comes first. We may object to this emphasis on rules, and we may use utilitarianism (even rule-utilitarianism) against it. But we cannot simply deny that insofar as utilitarianism is supposed to be a theory of morality, it puts its priorities suspiciously backward, deriving (or rejecting) rules on the basis of their consequences, rather than evaluating consequences in the light of the rules. Thus, some critics of utilitarianism insist that it is intolerably anarchistic, allowing for no essential social structures—in other words, no ethos—apart from the contingencies of utility.

Three further objections have been leveled against all of the various forms of utilitarianism:

1.   Different kinds of consequences may be extremely difficult to compare. Throughout our discussion, we have assumed the intelligibility of Bentham's first premise, that different units of "utility" (whether pleasure

and pain, happiness and unhappiness, or good and evil) can be placed on a similar scale and weighed. Mill is already suspicious of this, which is why he introduces the notion of "quality" of pleasure, allowing for different scales of measurement but thereby also destroying the simplicity and singularity of Bentham's calculus. But whether it is act- or rule-utilitarianism that concerns us, and whether actual or intended consequences of different courses of action are involved, is it at all clear that we can compare different values on anything like a similar set of scales? For example, suppose a city has a financial crisis and one of the suggestions for saving money is closing down the art museum and selling its contents. Closing down the museum may save the taxpayers thousands of dollars, but what is the cultural "cost" of doing so? Indeed, to speak of cost in this case already betrays one of the hidden assumptions of utilitarianism—that value in general can be placed on a general scale of *exchange,* with a single unit of exchange, namely, money. This may indeed be a valid assumption when we are wondering how many chickens we should sell in order to be able to buy a new barn. But when the less tangible aspects of human life are involved, we are rightfully squeamish about even trying to put a dollar value on them. There is something ethically discomforting about life insurance, however practically necessary such protection may be. There is something unsettling about buying and selling people's time and dignity in jobs that are a waste of time or just plain foolish. There is something unnerving about the art market and commercialized religion, not because money, art, and religion don't mix (gods have always demanded material sacrifices, for example), but because the values of art and religion—like our lives, time, and dignity—do not seem reducible to an exchange rate in dollar amounts. But even if we delete the financial currency of exchange implicit in the utilitarian formula, it would still seem "vulgar"—to use the insult Nietzsche used against Mill and his followers—to consider all pleasures and pains, all kinds of happiness and unhappiness, in the same scheme of things, even if qualified by an insistence on "quality."

2. The consequences of an act or a class of actions may be clearly positive and, nevertheless, the act is just as clearly wrong. Against act-utilitarianism, we have already considered the case of a single action (selling a decrepit used car and lying about it) in which the marginal utility of a "better" sale does not compensate for the lying and cheating that are employed to make that sale. But one might show that such examples are also true of an entire class of actions and thus operate against rule-utilitarianism as well. Suppose, for example, it could be

demonstrated that adultery would save more marriages than it would destroy and would make people more happy than miserable. Would adultery then be a moral act? Such research has often been attempted, but the results have generally been rejected, not because of lack of evidence but because such results violate our sense of morality. If adultery is wrong, as most people still believe, it does not matter whether it is conducive to happiness or not.

3. The most definitive objection to utilitarianism aims at the principle of utility itself. Mill protects the principle from abuse, for example, criticizing a very powerful man who makes himself happy at everyone else's expense, by insisting that "everyone counts for one and only one." The rule-utilitarian protects the theory against a gleeful sadist, for example, by insisting that it is not a single instance that is in question but a kind of action, namely, sadism. But even within this principle of equality and with the rule-utilitarian proviso, a serious ambiguity remains. Suppose a majority of the citizens of a town pass a tax law which, in effect, raises taxes for every member of a minority and, at the same time, cuts taxes for every member of the majority. Suppose, too, the majority members proudly announce their solution to the civic budget problem to financially pressed cities all over the nation, as a general means of balancing budgets. Leaving aside the difficulty of measuring amounts of pleasure and pain merely on the basis of dollar amounts, it seems clear that this act (and this type of act) is not wrong according to utilitarianism because it maintains utility and makes more people happy. And yet, we would probably all agree, the act is clearly unjust. Even good consequences do not compensate for injustice.

A second, more sadistic example favored by many critics of utilitarianism is this: suppose that a rather sick society gets great joy out of the spectacle of a few innocent people being tortured to death. Consider Rome during some of its darker days, for example. On the utilitarian account, the great joy of the spectators—if it outweighs the suffering of the few victims—is sufficient to make their behavior moral. Indeed, given a sufficiently large component of sadism in a population, this means of maximizing pleasure—if not minimizing pain—might be promoted as a national sport. But this, we object, would surely be unfair and immoral. This example, like the last one, shows that utilitarianism cannot take proper account of *justice*. The well-being of the majority is one thing, but justice may be something else. Happily, the two are usually commensurate. But, nevertheless, as an overall theory of the justification of morality, utilitarianism has been accused of failing a crucial test. It cannot provide adequate justification for some of our most important moral convictions.

KANT AND DEONTOLOGY

It is in reaction to the objections to utilitarianism that a great many philosophers have turned to an older tradition in which moral principles are not conditional on consequences or mere means to happiness, but absolute. In one sense, the origins of this theory go back to the beginning of human history, when the command of the chief, or the king, or God, was given unconditionally. One had an obligation to obey, regardless of the consequences. Whereas utilitarian theories ground morality in the pursuit of human happiness, these theories ground morality in the concept of *obligation.* We noted that such theories are *deontological* theories, from the Greek root *deon,* meaning "duty." In deontological theories, an act or a class of actions is justified by showing that it is *right,* not by showing that it has good consequences (though, again, it is usually assumed that right action will have good consequences). But unlike the unconditional obligations of ancient tribes or the unquestioning obedience of God's commands, the notion of right involved in deontological theories is not imposed or determined by any chief or king or divine being. These are obligations which we ultimately give *to ourselves.* The watchword of deontological theories, accordingly, is the all-important concept of *autonomy,* thinking and acting for oneself and doing what one knows is right.

The foremost modern defender of a deontological theory is Immanuel Kant. He was reacting to the early "utility" theories of Hume and other Enlightenment philosophers, and he anticipated the later objections to utilitarianism. (Kant wrote seventy years before Mill.) Kant insisted that what makes an act right or wrong cannot be its consequences—which are often entirely out of our hands and a matter of luck—but rather the principle (or "maxim") which guides the action. "Nothing . . . can be called good without qualification, except a *good will,* " he writes at the beginning of his *Grounding of the Metaphysic of Morals.* And having a "good will" means acting with the right intentions, according to the right maxims or principles, doing one's duty *for its own sake* rather than for personal gain or out of what Kant calls "inclination" (desires, emotions, moods, whim, inspiration, or sympathy). This is the heart of Kant's ethics, "duty for duty's sake," not for the sake of the consequences, whether one's own good or "the greatest good for the greatest number."

What is the court of appeal for deontological theories? The utilitarian, like the enlightened egoist and the Aristotelean teleologist, could appeal to actual human desires and aspirations. But deontological theory, because it is unconditional or absolute, rejects those desires and aspirations as the ultimate court of appeal—though, for Kant and almost all other deontologists, they nevertheless remain important. The court of appeal for a deontological theory is *reason*. Kant calls it "pure practical reason." Each of us is *rational;* that is, each of us has the ability to reason and arrive at the *right* way to act, by ourselves and without appeal to any "outside" authority. Each of us can figure out for ourselves what it is that we ought to do and not do. The authority necessary to justify morality is one's own moral autonomy. *To justify morality, therefore, is to show that it is rational, and to justify any particular moral principle is to show that it is in accordance with the principles of reason.* Morality, as we indicated in Chapter 1, is characterized by Kant as a system of *categorical imperatives,* that is, commands which are unconditional. We now appreciate better what this means; they are unconditional, not only in the sense that they apply to everyone without deferring to personal interests, but also in the sense that they are principles of reason and, as such, are not bound to the contingencies of life. They apply without regard to consequences. Kant takes this to be the heart of reason—that it envisions the world according to its own ideals and is not determined merely by the facts of the world.

Because moral principles are rational principles, according to Kant, their test must be purely *formal.* To prove that an act is immoral, it is not enough to show that its actual or probable consequences would be disastrous. One must demonstrate that its principle itself is "contradictory" and impossible. One of Kant's examples will serve as an illustration of what this means. Suppose I am considering borrowing money from you under false pretenses, by lying and telling you that I will pay you back next week (when in fact I will already be in Hawaii, never to return). The utilitarian would calculate the consequences (whether of the act or of the kind of act), but Kant insists that the act is wrong *no matter what the consequences.* What if, he argues, I were to apply the maxim of my act (that is, the principle upon which I am acting) to everyone else, and urge them to act similarly? Since morality is essentially a product of reason, I *must* be able to do this, for I cannot apply principles to myself alone. (The utilitarian would agree with this.) What would be the result? It would be to undercut the whole practice of promising to repay borrowed money, and if anyone were to ask, "Can I borrow some money and pay you back next week?" everyone would simply laugh. Such words would have become meaningless. Thus, Kant insists, the maxim contradicts itself in the sense that it could not be universalized as a principle of action for everyone without undermining the very possibility of performing such an action. This is not just to say that the consequences of generalizing the maxim would be disastrous. (A rule-utilitarian would agree with that.) It is a formal or logical inadequacy: the universalization of the maxim makes the action in question incomprehensible. For what would count as lying, in a community in which no one could ever be expected to tell the truth?

Notice that Kant's philosophy does not deny any reference or appeal to the consequences of an action. He makes no appeal to the actual consequences of an action—for who could know these before the action is carried out?—but he does include the intended consequences of the action in his formulation of the maxim itself. He also makes reference to the imagined consequences of the act or maxim universalized, so it would not be correct to say (although it is often said) that Kant rejects any appeal to consequences. But in comparison to the utilitarian's direct and often exclusive concern with consequences, Kant's ethics surely provides a distinctive contrast.

Part of what motivates Kant's deontology is a firm conviction that morality is something more than the customs and ethos of a particular society, something more than a set of sympathetic feelings we experience toward other people and other creatures. He believes—and wants to prove—that morality must be the same everywhere, built into the structure of the human mind just as the basic categories of truth and knowledge are. This is not to say that everyone everywhere in fact accepts all the same moral principles; neither do all people accept the principles of modern science (which Kant also insists are universal and necessarily true "for every rational being"). His argument is that every human being has the *faculty* of rationality, though not every human being actually cultivates and realizes that faculty. In effect, what Kant wants to do with his philosophy (as Aristotle wanted to do with his) is to help people cultivate their rational faculty by understanding better what it means to be moral and consequently becoming more moral. But he will readily admit that most people and most of the peoples of the world fall far short of his rational ideal.

The crucial point in Kant is his view that it is not just our personal "inclinations" that motivate us to act. There is a far nobler source of motivation, and this is reason itself. In other words, Kant thinks that egoism, enlightened or otherwise, is just plain false. We are not motivated only by self-interests. We are also motivated to act for the sake of reason alone. Thus the recognition that we have a duty need not be further supported by some realization of self-interest; it is enough that we recognize our duty, and because we are rational, we *want* to do it. This, too, is the meaning of the central notion of autonomy in Kant's philosophy. Not only can we think for ourselves and figure out what is right and wrong; we can also act contrary to our inclinations, including our most powerful desires and emotion, if they do not conform to the dictates of practical reason. It is this sense of autonomous, moral motivation, animated not by sympathy or by any other inclination but by "the moral law within," that makes Kant's ethics the most powerful defense of "pure" morality in the history of the subject.

This emphasis on "the moral law within" and the notion of autonomy is also at odds with the grounding of morality in "utility" or any other social concept. For Kant, morality is essentially an individual—as well as a universal—affair. It is individual in that, as an autonomous subject, everyone has both the ability and the duty to reason and figure out what is right. It is universal in that, because each of us is rational, the laws of reason and the principles of morality dictated by reason are necessary and shared by all of us. But what is left out of this polarity is the social fabric of an ethos, the sense of our being "social animals," as Aristotle defined us so long ago. This is not to say, of course, that Kant does not have a keen sense of community and the need for all of us to get along. Indeed, one of his "formulations" of the categorical imperative is that we should always act as if we were members of the perfect community, which he calls "the kingdom of ends." But it is doing our duty itself that is essential to morality. The good society, it is hoped, will follow. Morality is not as such a social concern, even though a good society obviously depends upon the morality of its citizens. Kant is well aware that societies as well as individuals can be immoral. But morals, therefore, cannot consist of the values and relationships within a society. Reason transcends all societies and dictates a set of rational principles which are to be obeyed by all.

Deontological theories such as Kant's succeed precisely where utilitarian theories fail—in showing how moral principles are unconditional and not dependent on utility, especially in those cases where

75

the greatest good for the greatest number can be realized through injustice or cruelty. It is not enough to show that society would be better served if one or two unfortunate but innocent individuals were put to death or tortured for the amusement of everyone else. Nor will it do for a society to benefit the majority at the expense of injustice to the minority, for there are moral claims which have authority even where the greater happiness is not served. Where the deontologist runs into trouble, however, is just where the utilitarian succeeds. We noted that one of the great attractions of utilitarianism is its emphasis on human happiness and well-being. The deontologist cannot be indifferent to such concerns, but, nevertheless, they clearly play a secondary role in the theory of morality. In one sense, we can understand the reason for this: morality must be grounded independent of personal inclinations (including the desire to be happy), for the inclinations are variable and undependable rather than not necessary and universal. And, in contrast to Kant's notion of autonomy, they are matters of "nature" rather than of a free and rational will. But is it possible or tolerable that happiness should be opposed to morality? To be sure, there are occasions in which we are obliged to do what we do not want to do. But could this opposition be general and mark an antagonism between doing right and living well as such?

This intolerable conclusion is precsiely what utilitarianism—and enlightened egoism—deny. If morality means doing our duty, and duty is separate from or opposed to what is in our own self-interest, how could the morally good person remain oblivious to happiness? Kant rejects this conclusion, insisting that we even have a duty to be happy. His odd reason is that an unhappy person is not in an optimum mood to carry out his or her duties. Furthermore, he says, rationality dictates that it would be most unreasonable to expect us to do our duty if there were no justice, no commensuration of goodness and happiness, no punishment for evil. But since it is obvious that we do not always find such justice in this world, Kant argues that its absence should rationally lead us to conclude that there must be justice elsewhere, in an afterlife, judged by an all-knowing and all-powerful beneficent God. Thus Kant, like many deontologists before him, ultimately ties his strict sense of morality and duty to religion, albeit a rational religion, one to be defended "through reason alone." But notice that Kant places religious belief on a moral foundation. He does not justify morality on the authority of God. In answer to

Euthyphro's question, he does not define morals in terms of religion but rather appeals both morality and religion to the authority of autonomous reason.

EXISTENTIALISM, EMOTIVISM, AND MOORE: WHY JUSTIFICATION?

In the preceding sections, we have primarily discussed two general types of ethical theory: teleological theories (including utilitarianism), strategies for justifying morality which appeal to the ultimate purposes and consequences of moral behavior, and deontological theories which appeal, rather, to the authority (especially the rational authority) of moral principles. We have also considered a number of particular courts of appeal, among them God's will, practical reason, the formal consistency of principles, the "design" of nature and human desires and aspirations, including selfishness as well as more enlightened egoism. For more than two thousand years, debate has raged over these strategies and the ultimate validity of such appeals, and ethicists will probably continue debating their various advantages and inadequacies for the next two thousand years as well. But there is another possibility, and that is that the entire enterprise of justifying morality and theorizing about its foundation is a mistake. Perhaps morality cannot be justified, or perhaps the attempt to justify morality already indicates some deep insecurity about morality, such that we are not convinced of its necessity without some proof or demonstration.

This insecurity can be detected even in the best defenders of morality. Some of the Sophists who are Socrates's interlocutors in Plato's dialogues offer persuasive arguments—that "might makes right," that justice is nothing but timid selfishness, that "man is the measure of all things"—and it is not entirely clear that Socrates refutes them. Aristotle warns us at the beginning of his *Ethics* that we should not expect more precision or proof than the subject allows and insists that there is no point in trying to convince people of the importance of the virtues if they have not already been brought up correctly to accept and practice them. Mill prefaces his "proof" of utilitarianism with the similar warning that one cannot really "prove" ultimate principles in ethics. Sometimes, however, the insecurity develops into full-scale skepticism. We have already noted that David Hume is such a moral skeptic. He did not believe that morality could be rationally defended, although he did defend a conception of morals based on certain universal, natural sentiments such as sympathy. Friedrich Nietzsche, on the other hand, not only thought that morality could not be rationally defended but argued that it was actually insidious, as we shall see.

Hume rejects the possibility of justifying morals (just as he rejects the possibility of justifying our knowledge of the world) because he thinks that there are no factual premises and no sound arguments that will yield moral judgments as their conclusion. Like many philosophers, Hume distinguishes sharply between *facts* and *values*, "is" and "ought" statements. How is it, Hume asks, that we feel justified in reasoning from some fact or facts about the world, e.g., that something feels good or makes us happy, to the judgment that one *ought* to do such and such? All such inferences, Hume suggests, are invalid. Morals, as we saw, are based on our sentiments, not reason, but the fact that we are so constituted as to be naturally sympathetic does not entail that we ought to be so, and thus hardly counts as a justification of morality in the strong sense demanded by philosophers. After all, if our sentiments were entirely different, so would be our morals. The question of which morals are "right" thus seems beside the point. It just happens that we are endowed by nature with certain sentiments (as it happens that we are endowed by nature with certain facilities for knowledge), and that's the end of it. Reason, alone, Hume argues, can neither motivate nor justify our behavior. And yet, Hume himself was a morally conservative citizen and did not advocate immorality. There is no justification for morality but neither is one needed.

Nietzsche, however, does not stop there. Not only is there is no justification for morality but there are some very good arguments *against* morality. Nietzsche asks why there should be so much emphasis on justification, if it is not because morality itself has lost its persuasiveness and we no longer believe in it. Traditional morality depends on the belief in God, Nietzsche surmises, and if people no longer believe in God as a moral force then wouldn't they also lose faith in the moral world order, perhaps without admitting it to themselves? Why the insistence on reason, he asks, if it is not because we fear our natural passions and aspirations, as if we need formal principles to keep our spirits in check. And why, he asks, this emphasis on universal principles, if not in order to impose the same set of bland demands and expectations on everyone, thus stunting the growth of those few who could excel far beyond the others? Morality, Nietzsche concludes, is not justifiable, not because philosophers haven't come up with a wholly acceptable justification, but because there is something seriously wrong with the very idea of "morality." Morality, Nietzsche argues, is a reactionary value system that rejects the virtues of strength and creativity and replaces them with such dubious virtues as meekness, humility, and innocence. The commands of morality are really a covert strategy for the protection of the weak. Morality, Nietzsche concludes, is not the noble aspect of our lives that we have pretended; it is rather a hypocritical expression of weakness.

An equally radical strategy is pursued by the French existentialist, Jean-Paul Sartre. He rejects the attempt to justify morality on the ground that any such justification will serve only to shift the ultimate responsibility for what we do away from our own free choice. Suppose a young man has to choose between joining the army to fight for his country or staying home with his grieving mother, who has already lost her husband and two sons in the war. What is the principle he should follow in making his decision? The fact is, Sartre argues, that he has to *make* a decision, and in doing so, he might endorse a number of principles (such as that one's primary obligation is to one's mother), but both the decision and its justification are nothing other than his having made his choice and having to live with it. We can see that Sartre takes Kant's insistence on individual autonomy to its extreme. Not only must we choose among alternatives and can we choose contrary to even our strongest inclinations; we are also responsible for determining what it is that is to count as right and wrong. The problem is thus not that of justifying morality. It is, rather, choosing to live in "good faith," which means, among other things, not falsely appealing to any authority, including reason, to support one's own free choices.

The rejection of the whole program of justifying morality has had its most radical and influential successes not in the flamboyant and passionate statements of Nietzsche and the existentialists, however, but in the sober academic pronouncements of English and American analytic philosophers of this century. The pivotal figure in this development was the Cambridge philosopher G. E. Moore, who shook up an entire tradition in ethics with his "Open Question Argument." The open question argument begins with a sharp distinction—as in Hume—between "facts and values" and then argues that value claims cannot be proven by any number of facts. One can always ask the "open question"—"Yes, but is it good?" Moore's own response to this conclusion was that "good" is the name of a "simple, undefinable, non-natural property" which we know by "intuition," thus giving rise to a theory, called "intuitionism," that one knows that something is good by simply "seeing that it is so," but without being able to prove it by appeal to the facts or by any abstract principle of reason. Moore argued that one cannot justify morality in the usual sense. That is, one cannot prove it by appeal to reason or purposes or consequences, but, nevertheless, one can know what is good. On that basis, Moore defended a version of utilitarianism. What he rejected was the traditional "proof" of utilitarianism—exemplified by Mill—in which good is identified with some natural property or widespread desire such as pleasure or prosperity.

Moore's followers were not so optimistic about their ability to intuit the good. They accepted his "open question argument" but rejected his intuitionism and utilitarianism. Some of them concluded that morality and ethics in general (as well as religion, aesthetics, and any number of other nonempirical disciplines) are devoid of substantial cognitive content. Attempting to justify them makes no more sense than trying to justify your preference for chocolate fudge ice cream. The leading movement in this wholesale rejection of ethics as such was *logical positivism*—a movement which had its origin among a number of German and Austrian philosophers and scientists who fled the Nazis in the 1930s. Their view of ethics was that opinions about values are mainly matters of emotion, not knowledge. The ethical theory developed by some of the logical positivists—notably by A. J. Ayer in England and C. L. Stevenson in the United States—was accordingly called *emotivism*. They argued—following Hume's argument—that value judgments cannot be based wholly on facts and that statements in ethics, therefore, are not matters of knowledge and cannot be justified as matters of fact. Thus, the general position of a great many contemporary philosophers has come to be called *noncognitivism,* which means that ethical statements are neither true nor false and cannot be justified as such.

Noncognitivism has had several variants in England and the United States in the past fifty years. Emotivism—the very strong noncognitivist view that making a moral judgment is logically on a par with yelling "Hooray" (A. J. Ayer's formulation)—was popular for a decade or so, but it ran up against a powerful objection, namely, it left little room for an adequate account of *moral reasoning,* that is, an account of how we deliberate and persuade ourselves and others of the rightness or wrongness of an action. This is essential to ethics, for, as we have seen, moral judgments consist not just of personal passions and preferences but of claims that at least purport to have rational, disinterested, objective status. To be sure, one can provoke emotion in other people through argument and one can persuade people through a variety of rhetorical and marketing devices, but the idea of justification drops out of emotivism and with it the claim that one's moral views are correct. Ideally, this might eliminate a good many moral disagreements, but it also eliminates the very moral judgment that motivated the logical positivists in the first place. If moral judgments are no more than expressions of emotion, then how does one argue with a fanatic, a Nazi, whose passions may be profound but whose opinions are immoral and intolerable? Whether or not morality is mainly a matter of reason, moral judgments require reasons. Noncognitivism, accordingly, gave up emotivism and shifted its attention back to the reasons we give to back up our moral claims.

Some undergraduates adopt a version of emotivism when they claim that "all value judgments are subjective" and dismiss any moral claim as "just a value judgment." But the difference between the noncognitivist and the undergraduate subjectivist positions is worth noting: the logical positivists and other noncognitivists developed elaborate theories of language and knowledge in support of their claim that ethics is not a matter of knowledge. The undergraduate subjectivist all too often uses only the glib conclusion and dispenses with the arguments and theories. The logical positivists defended their noncognitivism in order to root out much nonsense from the realm of moral discussion. Too many undergraduate subjectivists adopt the noncognitivist position as a way of avoiding criticism or worse, to avoid thinking about ethics at all. But, as many noncognitivists are now arguing, ethical claims nevertheless have their *reasons,* and ethics, even if subjective, nevertheless requires some objectively valid reasoning.

THE JUSTIFICATION OF MORALITY
AND THE PROBLEM OF RELATIVISM

Why are philosophers so concerned with the justification of morality? In part, they are concerned to know that what we do is right, and that we are justified in encouraging or forcing others (our children, immigrants, rebels, and deviants) to conform to our ways. This, of course, is just what Nietzsche rejects about it. With many social customs, we may be content merely to insist that "that's the way we do things here." We are perfectly willing to accept that people elsewhere—perhaps even our own children—do things differently. But where morality is concerned, as in such issues as sexual behavior and the treatment of children, we are not willing simply to accept these differences. The justification of morality is thus an attack on relativism—the view that different people have different moral systems and that no position is more correct than any other.

Thus, Kant asserts that morality consists of absolute, unconditional, "categorical" principles, and the utilitarians insist that there is, in fact, a single, universal standard by which all moralities may be judged, namely, the extent to which they do, or do not, maximize general happiness. The Judeo-Christian tradition eliminates the problem of relativism with the doctrine of one God and a single set of moral laws for every people. Plato and Aristotle, while recognizing the difference between their own values and the values of other cultures and classes, simply assumed that the values of Athenian aristocrats were superior to all others and saw no need to prove the point.

It is time to take a closer look at ethical relativism. Throughout most of the history of ethics, it was at best an eccentric thesis, defended on occasion by a few skeptics and some of the German romantics who were fighting against the moral imperialism of the English and the French during the eighteenth and nineteenth century. (Kant was obviously not one of them.) But today, at the end of the twentieth century, ethical relativism (like relativity in physics) is an inescapable thesis. With airplanes, television, and telecommunications, the world has gotten much smaller. Communities that were far apart in space and consequently in time are now neighbors, elbow to elbow, and the clash of differing mores and morals is commonplace. We are a "multicultural," pluralist society in which the differences between us are often more pronounced than similarities. The idea that what is right might vary from culture to culture and community to community thus becomes both more attractive and more repulsive. On the positive side, it encourages acceptance of differences and reduces friction. On the negative side, it aggravates disagreements and increases hostility. In ethics, our task is to understand what relativism claims and entails, and what it does not claim and entail. Is relativism a plausible thesis?

If we were to accept relativism, it is often argued, ethics in general and morality in particular, would be undermined. If "it's all relative," then what is the point of arguing for one moral position rather than another, unless it is for the practical purpose of winning someone to your side? But while this may serve a number of purposes, it does not count as a justification of morality, and the idea that there might be a number of different but equally correct moralities has often struck philosophers as a contradiction in terms. Either an act is moral, or it is not. The idea that an act could be moral in France and immoral in Japan thus embraces some basic confusion. Either it is *believed* to be moral in one place but not in the other—in which case at least one of them is wrong—or the difference is being misdescribed. Moral philosophers argue, for example, that although the superficial aspects of morals may differ from society to society, the deep structures of morals—for example, some version of "respect and human dignity" or "the pursuit of happiness"—are the same the world over. So, a comment or gesture might be a routine daily wisecrack in Paris but a sign of disrespect in Tokyo. The first would be moral (or at least, not immoral) and the second would be highly offensive and immoral. But the two acts are being judged according to the same shared value of "respect for others." It is just that what counts as respect is different in France and in Japan. Relativism, on this account, is a superficial thesis, describing superficial differences between societies. It does not, accordingly, present a threat to morality or make moral disagreements in principle unresolvable.

Some philosophers have argued the stronger thesis, that ethical relativism is, on the face of it, an absurd or self-refuting thesis. They claim that it is absurd or meaningless to say, "This is morally good in society X but not in society Y." So, too, some would say that it is equally meaningless to say that a factual claim in science is true for one society (e.g., pre-Copernican Europe) and false for another (e.g., the post-Einsteinian scientific world). Either something is true or it is not. Either something is morally good or it is not. If we drop the word "morally," of course, it makes sense to say that something is good for people in one society and not for another. A hot fire at night is good for Eskimos, but not so good in Cameroon. But to say that something is a moral issue seems to entail that there is a right or wrong answer, regardless of context. Thus we have (tentatively) followed Kant in his insistence that morality is universal. To say that something is immoral seems to be saying that this is *wrong*, not just "we don't like it" or "we don't approve of it." It might make sense to say that something is *considered* morally good in society X but not in society Y, but, again, the implication is that either one of them is wrong or there is some more basic, shared moral consideration that explains the difference. The real difficulties arise only when we insist that differences in morality are not just superficial but deep, a disagreement on the most basic principles and values.

There are at least two forms of relativism that often become confused in these discussions. There is ethical relativism, which concerns us here, and there is cultural relativism, on which ethical relativism is loosely based. Cultural relativism is a *descriptive* thesis, based on anthropological observation: different cultures do indeed have different ideas about what is right and wrong. Ethical relativism, on the other hand, is the view that what is *right* is relative to different cultures. The denial that there are any deep differences in moral matters among cultures is part of the cultural relativity debate. But, on the basis of anthropological observation of the past several centuries, it must be said that this denial is almost certainly false (though this demonstration is in the domain of empirical social science, and not an ethical question as such). Let us simply assume here that deep differences among cultures are an established fact. Not only do people get married in different ways and under different conditions; the very concepts of marriage and family are decidedly different in different cultures. Not only does what counts as stealing vary from culture to culture; the very notion of stealing is absent from some, extremely important in others. But, if these differences are true, does cultural relativism entail ethical relativism?

The answer, again, is no. One might well accept differences in various peoples' ideas of right and wrong and yet insist, as Kant did, that some of those ideas are just plain *wrong*. There is no paradox or self-contradiction here. One can accept the fact of diversity in morals without giving an inch to the thesis that one ought to have humility toward one's own moral prejudices and respect for others' values. Cultural relativism does not entail ethical relativism. Indeed, the visibility of the former may only reinforce a moralist's disdain for the latter.

Ethical relativism is itself an ethical thesis. It insists that we not only recognize moral differences but respect them too. Does this view embody a contradiction? If one asserts as a universal principle that everyone everywhere *ought* to respect ethical differences, one is indeed in an awkward position. The ethical relativist who asserts, as a universal principle, that "different things are considered good in different societies and therefore we *ought* to respect these differences" seems to be stating a contradiction, asserting as a universally correct principle that there are no universally correct principles. It is an obvious fact that not everyone agrees with that particular principle, the principle of tolerance. Of course, almost everyone is willing to tolerate slight differences, but when it becomes a disagreement over matters that are sacred or otherwise central to a culture's view of the good, tolerance quickly gives way to condemnation. How, then, should the ethical relativist deal with those who disagree? When the principle of tolerance is itself in dispute, it doesn't make much sense to limply say, "Oh, well, we simply disagree about that, but you're just as right as I am and I respect your opinion." On the other hand, it is no less paradoxical and absurd for the ethical relativist adamantly to insist that the opponent is wrong. According to whom? According to the relativist's relative standards? Certainly not according to the opponent's own standards.

The problem for the relativist is where to stand while pronouncing the doctrine that one moral view is as correct or incorrect as another. Is he or she living inside a particular culture, in which case the doctrine is certainly false? It may well be that killing one's grandparents by leaving them out on the ice is morally permissible and explicable in certain Eskimo cultures. But though one might be tolerant and argue that geriatricide is right in certain cultures in certain circumstances, this admission is not yet, in any sense, to weaken one's own belief that it is wrong to kill one's grandparents. Stepping outside one's culture, assuming that such a notion is even intelligible for most people, may allow us to say something like, "That's considered moral by them but not by Americans," but this is in no way to suggest that "one morality is as good as another." We have already stepped out of the moral context in which such comparisons are possible. (Note the Claude Levi-Strauss comment in Chapter 1, p. 15.)

To accept cultural relativism and to be an ethical relativist does not mean that one cannot compare moral systems, evaluate them, and choose between them. It certainly does not mean, as too many people take it to mean, that any culture and any ethics is as good as any other culture or any other ethics. In many cases, two systems will already include principles in common which can therefore be employed to judge one course of action morally better than another. If we disagree with the Australians about their treatment of aborigines, this is not a matter of ethical relativism. They have the same

85

principles of equality and fairness that we do; the dispute is one of politics and historical circumstances rather than a disagreement about basic moral values. If some ultimate good or purpose is shared by two cultures, that good or purpose may also be used to judge one moral system as better or worse. For example, if it were agreed by a communist culture and a capitalist culture (assuming that these are moral as well as economic systems) that the ultimate purpose of each culture is to make its citizens happy and materially comfortable, then there would be no question of ethical relativism, just the straightforward question about which system in fact makes people happier and more comfortable.

The real problem begins when ultimate principles and purposes clash. We need not go to the islands and jungles explored by anthropologists to see such a problem in progress, however. Consider the abortion issue in the United States. Even without bringing in the religious and legal/legislative dimensions of the dispute, it is clear that the ultimate principles, "right to life" and "individual choice," are in direct confrontation, even if both parties accept both principles and disagree only on their priority. But this often violent dispute should show us quite clearly which versions of ethical relativism make sense and which do not. It is easy to see how a person who is not very involved in the argument can listen to both sides and conclude that "they both have a point." The observer may even get involved and choose sides, pursuing one line of argument but not the other. But what the observer cannot say, except ironically, is that they are both right. Nor is it valid to conclude, because both sides are supported by powerful principles and strong arguments, that one moral position is as correct as another. So what is the relativist to say?

It is obvious that there are very intense and difficult disagreements in ethics, and if there is no general agreement about basic principles and their priorities there is no obvious forum for resolution. But this does not mean that two sides of such a debate can only stand opposed to one another, scream insults, and initiate legal suits. In the abortion debate, there is in fact considerable shared ground between the disputants, and a good deal of constructive talk and argument can take place on that shared ground. Once again, the essential thing is to appreciate the importance of providing reasons and support for one's ethical positions. This is not to say that our arguments should be dispassionate or passionless. Indeed, it is difficult to even think about an important moral issue without finding one's emotions already engaged. But mere conclusions—the sorts of slogans that find themselves on protest posters and bumper stickers—do not yet count as a moral position. And relativism in the lazy sense—"Oh, well, we disagree. Let's just avoid the issue"—is not a way of coming to grips with ethics. Mutual respect does not mean avoidance or cowardice. It means listening, carefully, to the opinions of those with whom one disagrees. It means cultivating and building one's own position and arguments to be ever more persuasive and convincing. And here we see the point of relativism, not limp acquiescence but genuine dialogue. Respect for one's opponent is not the same as accepting the opponent's view, nor does such respect in any way entail either giving up or weakening one's own view. Respect is not the same as agreement, though the naïve relativist and the vehement critic of relativism too easily confuse the two.

What about the case in which the principle of mutual tolerance itself is in question, that is, the issue of ethical relativism is itself the subject of ethical dispute? It is here that the ethical relativists find themselves in an impossible dilemma, and the conclusion does indeed seem to be that a relativist cannot consistently and coherently defend that position against someone who insists that morals are not relative, that is, despite the diversity of moral opinions in the world, there is nevertheless, a correct moral view—one's own, of course. But it does not follow, as many moralists have too quickly concluded, that ethical relativism itself is an incoherent position. It is not a coherent position applied to itself, but then, this is a common form of paradox throughout the logic of self-reference, but, ironically, it may have the desired effect in spite of its own impossible dilemma. When the relativist and the absolutist sit down to argue for and against relativism, they do in fact engage in just that dialogue and display just that mutual respect which the principle of tolerance demands.

At its best, ethical relativism is itself a moral view in which the principle of tolerance is the most important moral principle, at least where other cultures or communities are concerned. On the other hand, ethical relativism may be an excuse for not taking any moral position seriously, including one's own. Ethical relativism can be a strategy, a way of defusing ethical views, according to philosopher John Ladd. By answering a moral claim with the reply, "That's just your opinion," one robs it of its moral force and shifts attention from the moral claim itself to the person making the claim. In other words, it is a technique for dodging the moral issue. Relativism, in its indirect way, may be just as dogmatic and intolerant as moral absolutism, even while attacking dogmatism and intolerance.

Is morality ultimately justifiable? Or perhaps we should now ask, is *our* morality ultimately justifiable—where the scope of the *our* is itself in question? Ethicists often suggest that if relativism were true, then ethics would be impossible. At most, we could (like anthropologists) describe our morals, and we could continue to prescribe them, at least to one another. But we could not justify them. Our ethics would be without a foundation, and our prescriptions would be without an ultimate anchor. This fear, however, is unjustified. To think that the whole of morality turns on the question of justification and the threat of relativism is to turn ethics upside down. The process of justification may succeed from the top down, from the most abstract principles and purposes to the most particular moral judgments. But it does not follow, as many ethicists seem to believe, that the validity of the particular judgments depends upon their support from the more abstract principles discussed above. Whatever the strategy of moral justification, our moral lives proceed from the bottom up—from the ethos in which we were raised and in which most of us continue to live the whole of our lives. Indeed, it may be that we will never agree on even the formulation of the most abstract principles and purposes of morality, much less on their mode of justification. Nevertheless, within our culture, and apart from the exceptional clashes of morals, we do and will continue to agree on most of our day-to-day moral decisions and judgments. And as society expands, incorporating more and more former outsiders and coming into increasingly closer contact with other societies, the primary impetus of almost everyone is to "live and let live," finding a way to get along and live well together. Ethics does not depend on the success of philosophers finding an adequate justification for morality as a whole. The emphasis on justification gets confused with the importance of cultivating a coherent, well-thought-out view. The importance of appreciating differences and listening to the views of others gets replaced by the unnecessary and dangerous demand that we either prove them wrong or incorporate their views into our own thinking. It is the nature of justification that it always reaches further, for broader and better reasons. This is essential to ethics. But ethics is not just the quest for justification, and it is not essential or perhaps even possible to step outside of one's culture and find the one or three or ten principles that are or should be fundamental to every culture and every ethical viewpoint. Indeed, we might well ask, at this point, if our concern for morality as such has gotten too abstract, too far from our day-to-day concerns and values.

True, cultures collide, and, true, one can pursue these large questions about the role of autonomy and duty versus the place of self-interest and the public good in our conception of morality. But something is getting left out, a matter more personal than those addressed by these grand issues. It is, to put it in a banal phrase, our everyday notion of *a good person* and our daily concern for living well.

3

Living Well:
The Virtues and
the Good Life

Few people believe that morality is the highest goal or the sole purpose of life. Morality provides the constraints within which we enjoy ourselves, express ourselves, make friends and acquaintances, go looking for love, strive for success, and try to live our lives to the fullest. But ethics, ultimately, is about how to live and how to live well. It is not just concerned with the constraints imposed on us by morality. The questions that have been guiding us through Chapter 2 concern the nature and justification of morality. But these questions too often treat morality as a distinctive phenomenon, separated from questions of good fortune, success, and happiness. Perhaps we should ask instead, "How does morality fit into the good life?" Much of our discussion of morality thus far has tended to treat what we *want* and what we *ought to do* as antagonistic rather than complementary or mutually dependent considerations. Little has been said about what one should want and care about, about what sort of person one should strive to become. Properly understood, morality might not consist of a set of principles or rules of reason, might not require so much deliberation and calculation. It might be, instead, an intrinsic part of the good life, or the life well-lived. Such is the premise of a very different kind of moral theory, *virtue ethics*. On this view, living well, becoming successful, and being happy incorporate morality not as constraint, but rather as an aspect of the *virtues*.

Virtue ethics has been treated as a complement to traditional moral theory, and it has been defended as a radical alternative to traditional theory. The more moderate version insists only that traditional moral theory leaves something essential out of the account of our moral life, and virtue ethics will supply this. The more radical version insists that traditional moral theory has it all wrong, that questions of virtue and character undermine deontological and utilitarian theories and show their accounts of moral life to be bankrupt and their vocabulary of goodness and rightness to be misleading, if not fraudulent. Throughout most of Chapter 3, we will emphasize the moderate version of virtue ethics, as a supplement to the considerations concerning morality we examined in Chapter 2. But we will also discuss ways in which virtue ethics cannot serve just as a supplement but as an alternative to the other moral theory. In that regard we will look again at one of the most radical advocates of virtue ethics, the German philosopher Friedrich Nietzsche.

THE VIRTUES

The virtues are cultivated responses and actions that may require no deliberation whatsoever. Indeed, where deontology seems to require at least some deliberation in order for us to be acting on principle and utilitarianism encourages (even it does not require) the calculation of utilities, the expression or manifestation of a virtue seems to require little or no thought at all. One acts spontaneously. For example, the truly honest person never even *thinks* of lying. The virtues, accordingly, do not as such require deliberation. Indeed, too much deliberation—"Should I be generous? Am I supposed to leave a 20 percent tip or can I get away with less?"—is evidence that one does not really have the virtue in question. Many of the virtues would become ridiculous if they were preceded by the sorts of deliberation encouraged by moral theorists. One does not display a sense of humor by coming to the realization that one *ought* to laugh. Of course, some virtues involve moral principles and some require deliberative thought (e.g., being thoughtful), and a thoughtful person might well generalize about his or her virtues or formulate various self-reminders or "rules of thumb." ("I should try to be more generous.") But the virtues do not primarily rely on such thoughts and guidelines. Rather, the hallmark of a virtue is that it is engrained in one's character and, perhaps after years of cultivation and practice, seems perfectly natural.

The virtues tend to undercut the distinction between altruism and egoism that has so much preoccupied moralists and moral philosophers. A generous person may take delight in the well-being of others, but he or she need not do so. He or she may simply *be* generous, or one might say "overflowing," or take great pride in being a generous person. One can try to raise the objection that such prideful self-concern undermines or cancels out the generosity, but to be generous is simply to act and to be motivated by generosity; there is no further need to distinguish between self-interest and altruism. To say that a person has a virtue is not to invite an investigation into his or her motives or the consequences of virtuous action. If a person routinely acts courageously, one is justified in calling him or her courageous. And whether an act of courage has good or disastrous consequences for oneself or for others, it is, nevertheless, an act of courage. Of course, every such claim is nullified if one discovers some unexpected ulterior motive, but we need not dig into the depths of the soul and demand some purely virtuous or public-spirited motivation.

In Kantian moral philosophy, we examined in some detail the trouble with bringing together morality and happiness. These seemed at odds, or at least very different, and sometimes opposed, considerations that Kant ultimately conjoined only by an act of faith. Mill and the utilitarians, by contrast, defined the good in terms of happiness (or pleasure), but they then found themselves accused of leaving out the key concerns of morality. The emphasis on virtue and living well which we are about to explore does not separate the right and the good at all. It begins by assuming that we are social animals whose happiness is dependent on our getting along with others and our contributions to the community, and for whom self-esteem and self-respect are essential ingredients in our well-being. Our well-being, accordingly, is tied to how others think of us and how we think of ourselves. Our self-interest, if we want to use that term so generally, most often depends on being thought well of by others and being able to think well of ourselves. What makes us think well of ourselves is knowing that we are doing what we are supposed to do, not just in the sense of conforming to the rules or making our marginal contribution to the community, but by being an admirable sort of person, liked and respected by others. Doing right and making ourselves happy are one and the same. The conflict of duty and self-interest is not the conceptual key to ethics, but a personal problem that comes from an inadequate conception of self. According to Aristotle, the virtues are not merely a means to happiness, but an essential part of happiness.

A virtue, according to Aristotle, is an *excellence*, a character trait that is essential to happiness, getting along with other people, and living well in general. A virtue, according to Socrates, is knowing and doing the right thing for the good of one's soul. A virtue, according to David Hume, is a special trait of character that is pleasing both to other people and to ourselves. These differences in definition already indicate the presence of considerable disagreement, even among those philosophers who would endorse the virtues as central to ethics. Is a virtue to be defined in the context of a particular society with its particular needs and values, as Hume suggests? Or is it strictly a matter of individual integrity, as Socrates argued in the *Crito*? Aristotle says that a virtue is an excellence and often compares the various virtues to the skills and talents of a craftsman or a physician; certainly a great many virtues require considerable skill, and virtually all of the virtues require cultivation and practice. As varied as these definitions are, we can safely say that a virtue is a desirable trait of character. What kinds of traits are virtuous and what makes them desirable are at this point open questions.

Honesty is a virtue. So is courage. But charm and wit and a good sense of humor also seem to be virtues, and these do not seem to be the same sort of virtue. Perhaps we should draw some sharp distinction between moral virtues—such as honesty—and nonmoral virtues—such as wit. One might suggest that the moral virtues exemplify a kind of duty, and thus fall under a deontological analysis. Nonmoral virtues, on the other hand, are traits that are pleasing or popular, features or abilities that are useful or amusing, characteristics that have nothing to do with duty and seem to be morally optional, but nonetheless make a considerable contribution to the general happiness. Thus nonmoral virtues would seem to be prone to utilitarian analysis, and they are virtues insofar as they contribute to general happiness and well-being. Thus all of those personal features that lend themselves to civility and getting along with other people would be nonmoral, utilitarian virtues: politeness, hospitality, tactfulness, an even temper, congeniality. Only those virtues that are obligatory and fall under a general moral rule would be properly called moral virtues.

The problem with this approach is that the virtues do not divide up all that neatly into two categories, and we run the risk of falling back into the dispute between deontologists and utilitarians, we will most likely lose whatever advantages virtue ethics has to offer us. Many virtues—e.g., loyalty and generosity—seem to be ambiguous in the terms of the ongoing moral debate between Kantians and utilitarians. Are these moral virtues or not? Is a person who is disloyal acting immorally? To be sure, a person who refuses to stick with a friend, a colleague, or a company that is committing a serious crime might be said to be choosing morality over loyalty, but how are we to understand loyalty and disloyalty as such? Loyalty, unlike honesty, is tied to particular people or institutions. There is no intelligible imperative that says "Be loyal to everyone." One can be loyal only to those with whom one is already engaged in one form or another. But then, is loyalty to be understood in terms of a specific, acquired duty, like promise-keeping, as if loyalty were an implicit obligation or commitment? To be sure, loyalty may involve obligations, but to call loyalty an obligation seems to go against the spirit of the virtue, which seems different from obligation and more like love, affection, and friendship, a kind of attachment and not a duty. So, too, if a person is ungenerous, does not give to charities, and regularly under-tips waiters and waitresses, would we say that he or she is immoral? Probably not, unless, perhaps, he or she were also a hypocrite, urging others to be generous and even make sacrifices while refusing to make them personally. Honesty, on the other hand, does seem to lend itself to moral judgment in a straightforward way. Lying is immoral. But there are many forms of honesty, telling the truth when asked, for example, and volunteering the truth when necessary. The former seems like a duty, but the latter does not. Honesty may be optional—you are not obligated to tell your roommate that her new sweater simply looks awful. Honesty may serve an important purpose and further the happiness of others, but not be an obligation. Indeed, honesty can even be a vice, not a virtue at all, such as when one uses painful truth to humiliate and embarrass, to break up friendships, and intentionally cause harm to others.

A virtue may be such that it fulfills no obligations and does not matter to the public good at all, except by way of its effect on observers. Much of what we call restraint and moderation or what Aristotle called temperance are virtues that have to do with one's desires. Consider, for example, the glutton. The glutton eats too much, may well embarrass him or herself at the dinner table, and embarrass his or her friends and family as well. Gluttony is a vice, and the very opposite of moderation. But the vice is the gluttony itself, the excessive desire for food. It is not essential that the glutton acknowledges his or her gluttony, nor it is essential that he or she be embarrassed. Indeed, we will probably think gluttonous behavior all the more disgusting when it is utterly shameless and unrecognized as such on the part of the glutton. Nor does the vice of gluttony depend upon its effect on other people. The glutton becomes no less gluttonous by sneaking snacks and restricting the gluttony to the privacy of his or her own kitchen. Nor is gluttony a vice and moderation a virtue because the latter is healthy and the former detrimental to good health. Good health may be the reward of being virtuous, and being overweight and in ill-health may be two of the costs of the vice, but gluttony would remain a vice even if the latest medical headlines suggested that overeating can be good for you. What constitutes gluttony is the rapacity of one's desire for food. What constitutes the virtue of moderation, on the other hand, is not holding back or resisting temptation so much as it is having less excessive desires in the first place. *The virtue, in other words, has much more to do with what kind of a person one is than what one does.* It has only secondarily to do with its effect on others—although no doubt one of the reasons that gluttony is a vice is because it disgusts other people. And it has little if anything to do with duty or obligation—unless, perhaps, one has promised not to be gluttonous. Gluttony and moderation seem to have nothing to do with rational principles in the sense Kant describes, and they have wholly to do with what Kant called the inclinations. The glutton does not lack or fall short of any moral principle. He or she is simply a pig. Wanting too much makes a person repulsive. There need be nothing deontological or utilitarian about it.

Of course, gluttony seems even more repulsive to us when it is combined with poor social skills and lack of consideration for other people, and it gets even worse when we think of the millions of people in the world who are starving. One can always bolster the criticism of a vice by bringing in consequences and considering the effects on others, but it would be a misunderstanding of vice and virtue to think that the social implications or consequences alone are significant. There are excesses of desire that do not affect other people at all, but, nevertheless, we think less of the person who indulges in them. Our language of disapproval here is significant, however. We do not generally use the language of right and wrong, much less of morality, and nor do we use the cost/benefit language of utilitarianism. We use critical terms such as "repulsive" and "disgusting," or we express our repugnance through terms of amusement, disdain, and ridicule. So, too, we talk about the virtues not so much in terms of their goodness or rightness but rather in terms of their being desirable or admirable traits. The traditional language of the good and the right, whether applied to people or actions, strongly suggests and invites deontological or utilitarian evaluation. But the language of admiration and disgust gets us right to the heart of virtue ethics, and such talk seems to be much more the substance of our daily moral commentary than the employment of moral principles or utilitarian calculation.

The distinction between moral and nonmoral virtues is less important than it would seem to be from a deontological point of view. Yes, there are virtues that can be understood as instantiations of a moral principle, but it would be a mistake to think that all of them are. Yes, there are virtues that are mandatory and not at all optional, but it would be a mistake to think of all virtues in terms of duty or obligation. From the point of view of what one considers admirable or desirable, whether or not a virtue is an instantiation of a moral principle or a matter of duty or obligation may well be of secondary importance. Many people seem to consider loyalty more important than morality, for example, when they argue "my country right or wrong" or when they severely chastise their friends for abandoning them in favor of their moral principles. People seem to forgive even straightforward immorality—for example, Robin Hood's thievery—if it is done in the name of generosity, a virtue. From the point of view of virtue ethics, morality is secondary to personality. This is not to say that you can be immoral if only you are sufficiently charming, nor is it to deny that conformity to moral rules is an essential aspect of character. But in virtue ethics a person does what he or she does because that is the sort of person he or she is, whether or not there is an appropriate moral principle to conform to.

Utilitarianism does not take the distinction between moral and nonmoral issues all that seriously. It is more concerned with the maximization of happiness and the general good. Like virtue ethics, utilitarianism subsumes moral categories under a more general concern that does not take great pains to distinguish between what is morally right and what is good for other reasons. Thus honesty is generally good because it prevents harm and lying is usually wrong because it does harm. But in a like manner, a sense of humor is generally good because it increases the amount of happiness in the world and the lack of one is bad because a person without humor is not only less likely to enjoy life but very likely to dampen the enjoyment of others as well. In virtue ethics, however, it is not harm and happiness that are primarily at stake but rather the praiseworthiness of a certain trait of character. Honesty is admirable, not because it is conducive to the greatest good for the greatest number or because it is a duty but because it is in itself commendable. A sense of humor is a good thing to have not because it makes you or other people happy (and it is certainly not a duty to laugh) but because it is in itself admirable.

Such explanations are incomplete, however, and as stated will certainly raise more questions than provide answers. Why should honesty and a sense of humor be commendable? Why not instead clever prevarication and dour seriousness? What does it mean to say that honesty and a sense of humor—or loyalty, generosity, and moderation—are in themselves admirable or commendable or desirable? Virtue ethics will not succeed at accounting for our moral life if it cannot back up its estimations of worth. Why are some traits virtues and other traits vices? At least deontology and utilitarianism give us answers to this question.

We can begin to answer this question by looking at the role virtues play in the living of a meaningful, fulfilling life. A virtue alone is no virtue. To be honest just for the sake of being honest or loyal just for the sake of being loyal is obstinacy, not virtue. It can even be perverse. (Imagine telling your best friend that he is laughably short, which is true, but need it ever really be said?) Thus we need to link the virtues together and to think of them not as isolated traits that are good in themselves, but as contributions to an overall conception of character. In Aristotle, this leads to an ambitious, but ambiguous, thesis known as *the unity of the virtues*. The gist of the thesis is that you don't really have any virtue if you don't have all the virtues. Thus an honest man will be loyal and generous as well. The idea behind the thesis is that a virtue should not be a personality quirk but an essential part of an overall good character. Aristotle assumes that there is one general virtue underlying all of the other virtues: good judgment (or what he calls *phronesis*). What the thesis ignores or avoids, however, is the unfortunate fact that our virtues, like our moral principles, can and do sometimes come into conflict. A soldier or employee who is ordered to lie by a superior officer or manager is torn between the virtues of honesty and obedience. A friend who is asked to lie by a friend is torn between the virtues of honesty and loyalty. A host who watches a guest abuse the dog and drop ashes on the new leather sofa experiences obvious discomfort in spite of his virtues of toleration and hospitality. Moreover, as Nietzsche in particular argued, the vigorous pursuit of one virtue may in fact eclipse or interfere with the cultivation of others, as when an artist pursues his or her creativity beyond acceptable social boundaries or a politician pursues his or her leadership abilities into the twisted corridors of power. In all of these cases the virtues seem to be a disunity rather than a unity.

VIRTUE AND THE VIRTUES

Individual character and personal virtue are tied up in a whole way of life, or ethos. We invite disaster when we assume that virtue is virtue, that what is admired in one context will be admirable in another, and we similarly invite disaster when we look only at particular virtues and ignore the life in which they play their part. Moral principles may be sufficiently broad in their application to invite such abstraction and generalization, and the principle of utility by its very nature is designed to apply to every situation in which there are sentient beings with their preferences and their interests, but virtues tend to be more specific. Because of the convoluted history of morals, the term *virtue* has become ambiguous. On the one hand, a virtue is a particular feature of a person's character, such as honesty, wittiness, generosity, or social charm. This is the sense in which we are using that term here, and, accordingly, we will typically indicate the plural, *virtues*. On the other hand, *virtue* is used as an all-encompassing term; we speak of a person's virtue or talk of virtue in general, using the word as a synonym for *morality*. Kant, for example, uses the word virtue in exactly this way. Of course, a person who has virtues will very likely be virtuous, and a virtuous person will no doubt have at least some virtues. Nevertheless, the two conceptions are distinct.

Virtue and the virtues need not go hand in hand. A person may have many virtues, but nevertheless lead such a wild and unconventional life (even with no immoral behavior) that we could not call that person virtuous. On the other hand, a person, perhaps out of fear of punishment and general inhibition, may well live a life that is wholly virtuous in the moral sense, and yet be an utter bore. His or her moral character may be unblemished, but we would not necessarily regard the person as virtuous. An account of his or her life may well be pathetic. For example, the British novelist Jane Austen often creates characters who are perfectly and self-consciously proper, but they have no sense of humor or vitality whatever, and the main aim of her hero-ine is to avoid an impending marriage to such a proper, but utterly dull man. Morality or the moral virtues alone, in other words, do not necessarily produce good character, and in the absence of other, clearly nonmoral virtues, they may even be a vice. The most admirable people may lead morally ambiguous lives, and some indisputably moral people may nonetheless be impossible to like or admire.

If one is not willing to put the virtues ahead of morality, one might decide that the virtues are subject to moral constraints. A deon-tologist might adopt virtue ethics as a complement to duty and autonomy, admitting that the virtues are what make social life livable and that they define what we consider to be good character, but only within moral parameters that are not themselves matters of virtue. In this view, virtue might be thought of as social skills and entertaining or useful social habits, which the deontologist might well admit are necessary to being a good person. Indeed, the deontologist might also concede that there is no warrant for enforcing any sharp distinction between moral and nonmoral virtues. Honesty as a virtue is not merely an instantiation of the duty to tell the truth and, as a virtue, it need not be considered necessarily moral. But, whatever the virtue, it must be morally acceptable. An exceptional ability to charm and swin-dle the shirt off of unsuspecting strangers could not be a virtue, no matter what the context, just as the ability to kill children with a sling-shot could not count as a virtue, even if it were admired or enjoyed by some particularly demented sub-group of society. Thus, the deontolo-gist might well accept a moderate view of virtue ethics, adding only the stipulation that virtue must conform to or at least not conflict with morality. So, too, the utilitarian might insist that a virtue, whatever else its features, must advance or at least not retard general well-being. Both the deontologist and the utilitarian could agree that the virtues are important and are to be understood independent of duty and utility respectively, but they would insist that morality and the public good are, nevertheless, primary.

This compromise position on the role of virtue in ethics, however, does have a drawback. Requiring that a virtue should not be immoral or harmful renders the concept of virtue secondary and inessential to ethics. This view declares that virtues are good things to have because they are pleasant or congenial or enjoyable or even exciting, but they are as such only embellishments and details in our moral life, subject to the constraints of morality and the interests of utility. A more radi-cal position on the virtues is that they are desirable for their own sake and do not depend on morality and utility for their legitimacy. They may even conflict with morality and utility. The point is not that good citizens should be something more than dull rule-followers. The point is that admirable people are something more than moral or useful.

Nevertheless, what counts as a virtue certainly depends on the nature of the society in which it is embedded as well as on the overall character in whom it plays a vital role. Hume may be correct in saying that a virtue is a feature that is particularly pleasing and desirable to others, but what is pleasing and desirable depends on the nature of the context and the culture of the society in question. What was pleasing to Hume and his gentlemen friends in Edinburgh were, understandably, the virtues of a gentleman. What was pleasing to Agamemnon on the battlefield in front of the walls of Troy was a set of virtues that were certainly not gentlemanly. The fact that a virtue must be considered admirable within the context of one's particular society means that the virtues may well vary from context to context, whether they serve some specific practical function, such as having good business sense in the corporate world or knowing how to handle snakes on a snake farm or whether they appeal to the general ideals of a culture. Being devout and faithful will be among the greatest virtues in a religious society. Being creative and even eccentric will be virtues in a society of artists or academics in which originality and individuality are conducive to creativity, while being honorable and acting honorably will be among the highest virtues in a society such as Japan, in which proper behavior is often precisely described and public shame may be worse than death.

Virtues can also become outmoded. Being able to fight well with a sword and being "the fastest gun in the West" are no longer virtues in twentieth-first century America. At most, they might be salable skills in Hollywood. Having the talent to be a crack computer programmer would not have been a virtue during the Trojan War and having a superb sense of humor would not have been a virtue in a medieval Carmelite monastery. The aging of virtues is almost always resisted and deplored as a loss of values, but as societies change (not necessarily for the better) the virtues will tend to change too. What once was a virtue may well become a vice, and what was a vice for one generation may well become a virtue for the next.

Philosophers have often argued that morality is defined in part by its universality, but few ethicists have been tempted to say that about the virtues. Indeed, the most striking thing about the virtues is how they vary from culture to culture and through history. Many

Americans value a sense of humor, comedy, and a good laugh, but in some other societies humor is less important and raucous laughter is considered both foolish and obnoxious. Americans, on the other hand, generally tend to avoid discussions and rituals having to do with death, but in many cultures the dead and ideas about death play a large part in daily life. The ancient Egyptians, for example, had elaborate daily rituals concerning death. In America, people in mourning are often ignored or merely tolerated, and if the mourning process goes on very long, the person in mourning may be criticized or sent to seek psychiatric help. In other societies mourning may be expected to last a lifetime and the American attitude might be considered irreverent and pathological. (This is the accusation, for example, in Ernest Becker's *Denial of Death* and in Martin Heidegger's insistence that *Being-toward-Death* is an important aspect of the human condition.) Thus the capacity to mourn for a substantial amount of time is a virtue in some societies and is not a virtue (or is less of a virtue) in others.

To understand why this is so, we need to look at the overall social context. Death is an ineradicable aspect of the human condition. But what most Americans mean by death, whatever their religious convictions and beliefs about the afterlife, is quite different from the idea of death in those societies that emphasize death in mourning rituals. For many Americans, death is considered an individual or family tragedy. In many other societies, death is also a social misfortune and part of the predictable ebb and flow of communal life. One may lament the lack of community and larger family-feeling among many Americans and criticize the lack of comprehension and compassion concerning death that an absence of established mourning rituals may indicate. But the absence of certain virtues regarding death (for which we do not even have names) is part of an overall conception of life, and one cannot criticize the virtues (or the lack of them) without taking that conception into consideration.

The virtues are part of a way of life. To suppose that the virtues are the same the world over is to presume that life is the same and all people consider the same things important and valuable. Even where universal aspects of the human condition are in question, societies and significance vary enormously. Everyone has to eat, but they eat very different foods in very different ways and attach very different significance to eating. A delicacy in one culture is taboo in another. What counts as gluttony or bad manners in one society is considered to be polite and appreciative behavior in another. Almost all societies reproduce themselves, but even the act of reproduction has very different and usually very complex meanings and constraints in different cultures and, accordingly, is associated with very different virtues and vices. (In what kind of culture, for example, could a person have the virtue of being "a lover"?) Even where the activities are in some sense similar and equally necessary, in other words, we expect to find significant differences. And when we begin talking about the sacred and essential conventions of a culture, those having to do with religion and status, for example, we can expect considerable and sometimes violent differences in the understanding of the virtues. To take but one example which we will explore in some depth shortly, the virtues of an aristocratic society, in which a certain superiority is presumed and the necessities of life are taken care of by others, are going to emphasize very different virtues than a society that is egalitarian, at least in theory.

But surely there are some common, nonrelative virtues, if only those that are essential to the survival and stability of society as such. But even here, we find significant differences. Cooperativeness would seem to be such a virtue, but the very idea of a free market system would seem to highlight the very opposite virtue, competitiveness. Of course, a free market presupposes a certain amount of cooperation, but the point is that even the basic virtues of congeniality and getting along together can be understood in very different ways. So, too, with such seemingly universal virtues as courage and generosity. Courage in Homer's Greece could be measured by one's stalwart behavior in hand-to-hand combat, and even Aristotle insists that the only true measure of courage is on the battlefield. In twenty-first century America we most often mention courage in the context of the "courage of one's convictions" or in the context of a patient coping with a terrible disease. That is hardly the same virtue as the courage of Achilles facing a hundred Trojans in battle. Generosity in modern societies with rich philanthropists may refer to an overflowing of wealth that spills out to feed the hungry and help the needy and put on art exhibits and operas. In medieval society, generosity required considerable personal sacrifice, as when Thomas Beckett gave away everything he owned to the poor. And among some Native American tribes generosity was expressed in the ritual of *potlach,* a competition to see who can give away more than anyone else as a matter of status and honor. Does one need to make a considerable sacrifice to be generous? Do these three examples reflect the same notion of generosity? The same virtue? Again, to adequately understand the virtue, one needs to take the overall social context into account. But even considering the similarities and differences among societies, the idea that there is one overriding rule or measure seems implausible at best.

To get a concrete idea of at least one well-developed catalog of virtues, let us consider the well-known list that comes from Aristotle. His list reflects the virtues of Athenian society at a particular moment in its history. It is important to keep in mind that Aristotle's Athens was no longer the Greece of Homer's *Iliad*, that the Athenians were no longer a crude tribe in conflict with other crude tribes. Athens was a *polis*, a free and sophisticated city-state, at least when compared with any other society in ancient history—with a representative government and a rich heritage of art, philosophy, and statesmanship. Aristotle's list of the virtues sums up the Athenian notion of honor, which includes being held in high public esteem for one's civility and debating virtues, as well as for always acting in such a way that one's good name will never be challenged. This is a very different conception of virtue from the warrior virtues of the *Iliad*, in which physical domination rather than successful civility was the measure of one's public status. Achilles and Agamemnon, two heroes of the Trojan War, would have been considered barbarians in Aristotle's Athens.

Here is Aristotle's list of virtues:

Courage	Friendliness
Temperance	Truthfulness
Liberality	Wittiness
Magnificence	Shame
Pride	Justice
Good temper	

One of the first things we may notice about this list of virtues is that it includes some virtues which we should not consider as such: pride, for instance. We often think of pride as a kind of egoism, or at best as a kind of defensiveness. The closest we come to understanding Aristotle's virtue is in our accusation, "Have you no pride!" But Aristotle obviously means more than the unwillingness to humiliate oneself. To be proud is to have self-esteem, but it is not just to feel good about oneself, as we might say; it is to see oneself as superior—because one *is* superior. Without being smug or condescending, one should fully acknowledge and enjoy one's status and respect in the community. It is different today. Undergraduates who do superb work or perform brilliantly on an exam should not feel embarrassed about it before their classmates. But neither should they act superior on that account. So, too, our politicians and leaders today must walk a delicate line between their leadership abilities and their power on the one hand and the requisite sense of humility on the other. Aristotle's fellow Athenians would not consider humility a virtue at all, but rather, a vice, a sign of weakness or insipidness.

Aristotle's list also omits certain cardinal Christian virtues, faith and hope, for example. Charity is, in a way, included in liberality, but that is quite different from the Christian virtue. Liberality is overflowing, self-sufficiency coupled with abundance. Charity by contrast is a virtue of self-sacrifice and a keen awareness of our connection to the poor. Magnificence (which would include hosting great parties) may be a welcome virtue, but it is not the same as amiability and hospitality in our much more private and personal sense. A good temper may be a desirable virtue in a neighbor who is armed with a sword, but it is not the same as the warmth and good neighborliness that many Americans expect today. Indeed, it is probably safe to say that a modern American visitor to ancient Athens would very likely be appalled by the society we have so idealized and idolized for so many centuries. We would not recognize many of the Aristotelian virtues as virtues at all.

The names of the virtues are often misleading, not only because of the usual difficulties of translation but also because of the vast difference between the context and culture in which these virtues and their names took part and our own. Temperance, for example, does not refer to abstinence but only to moderation. Indeed, Aristotle and his friends would have looked upon someone who refused on principle to indulge in wine, sex, and song as an insufferable bore. And friendliness for Aristotle is not at all our slap-a-stranger-on-the-back-and-give-a-big-smile variety. Friendliness refers more to *being* a friend than to any particular feeling or expression of friendship. It certainly does not mean being friendly to everybody.

Aristotle sometimes says that the good man has *all* the virtues, indeed, that one cannot have any of them without having all of them. His claim for the unity of the virtues may be overstated, but we can accept that the virtues are often interrelated. He also says that virtue develops from a certain good upbringing and self-control. The virtues in general, he argues, are "means between the extremes," and one must be raised to have the right perceptions, good judgment, as well as to perform the right actions. To know the means between the extremes is, for one thing, to have and to act on the correct amount of emotion or desire. For example, temperance involves a moderate but not negligible amount of desire, while gluttony involves much too much desire and abstemiousness too little. Courage is the mean between cowardice and foolhardiness, where cowardice is having too much fear and foolhardiness too little. Notice that, on this account, courage is not the same as fearlessness. Indeed, fearlessness, of the sort depicted in many American movies, would be considered by Aristotle to be either foolhardiness or wishful fiction. A virtue, he says, "is a state of character." That means that it is not just an isolated trait or feature of our behavior, however benign. It is not merely doing the right thing at the right time, and it is not merely a passing passion. For Aristotle, a virtue must be drilled into us along with all of the other virtues since childhood and such that it is now a matter of habit. Indeed, the idea that a person should struggle to act virtuously would strike Aristotle as nonsense; to have a virtue means that one acts virtuously naturally, without struggle or moral turmoil. The test of virtue, according to Aristotle, is that one enjoys its exercise. It is no virtue when a person forces himself to do something. Furthermore, the virtue and its exercise fit in and go along with all of the other virtues as well. Aristotle has in mind an ideal he learned and borrowed from Plato, the harmony of the soul. Harmony requires coherence, not conflict, and the most obvious way to have a coherent, harmonious soul is to have all the virtues in a single package, cultivated in us as second nature since childhood.

The idea that virtue is primarily a matter of good upbringing and second nature as well as the ideal of harmony marks an important shift away from traditional moral theories. Of course, no deontologist or utilitarian would deny the importance of moral education, and the utilitarian, at least, would absorb the ideal of harmony under the heading of happiness. But Aristotle's virtues are formulated around a certain kind of life. Ethics is a question of one's whole character, and not just a question of this virtue or that. And because they are part of a particular way of life, these virtues and the happiness they yield are not available to anyone. Indeed, Aristotle thought that barbarians could not have any of the virtues because they did not grow up and live in so sophisticated a society as the Greek polis. He might well think that of us too.

The virtues listed by Aristotle are the virtues of well-educated, aristocratic, male Athenian citizens. Women in Athens did not have the freedom, the education, or the status to strive for such ideals. Slaves, of course, could be nothing more than "good slaves," according to Aristotle. Children were not to be called virtuous or happy; they were pre-adults, whose virtuousness and happiness could be judged only later. Because Aristotle was an aristocrat who disdained physical labor and depended for the necessities of life on those who had to perform the demeaning tasks of providing them, he ignores the virtues of hard work and perseverance. He expresses nothing but scorn for what we would call the commercial virtues, or the virtues of business, and he would have considered much of the protestant work ethic and what Americans consider success to be depraved. So, as appealing as it may be to some, the prospect of simply adopting Aristotle's conception and list of the virtues is neither plausible nor politically possible. What we can do, however, is to return to the heart of Aristotle's ethics, appreciate how his conception of the virtues developed out of the practices and traditions of his society, and develop a conception of the virtues that is appropriate to modern democratic society.

VIRTUES AND VICES: PRACTICES AND TRADITION

Virtues tend to be more or less specific to certain practices and traditions. Aristotle's list of virtues is quite explicitly limited to that small class of male Athenian aristocrats whose role in the polis was leadership and statesmanship. There were other virtues for ordinary soldiers and for craftsmen, for wives, for slaves, and for farmers. The virtues, obviously, were not only good in themselves and desirable for their own sake. They were functional. They served a purpose in the society in which they played a part. This is not necessarily to say that they served the general utility, for societies may have purposes quite apart from matters of utility or the public good, and it need not be true that those purposes or their realization make people happier or give them pleasure or satisfy them in any obvious way. But in the concepts of function and purpose we have at hand a large part of our answer to the question, what makes a virtue a virtue. We do not need to appeal to either general rules of morality or to considerations of utility and general welfare. We should rather look to the ideals of a particular society, what inspires and ultimately motivates its most admirable members.

In his book, *After Virtue*, Alasdair MacIntyre provides us with an extensive analysis of the concept of virtue and the variety of virtues that we find in history from Homer to the Victorians. A virtue, he tells us, is not merely an admirable trait in a particular society. It is, rather, one of the cardinal features of a *practice*, a specific goal-oriented activity that carries with it a certain tradition, an established way of doing and thinking about things. As we discussed in Chapter 1, a game of chess might be an example of such a practice. Chess is a practice that has evolved over centuries. When you sit down at a chess board with a friend, you do not invent the rules or the goals of the game; they are already there for you, along with the pieces and their desig- nated moves and a long tradition of tried and sometimes true strate- gies for winning. What we might call the virtues of a chess player, accordingly, are determined by the strategic nature of the practice. We can imagine a tradition in which that practice and its virtues would be very different, for example, if the object of the game were to shoot the tops off the pieces with shotguns, but within that practice and tra- dition that we call chess the goals and the virtues of the game are quite clear and thoroughly settled.

What we have called an ethos is a combination of various prac- tices and traditions, cultivated over time and defining certain virtues as especially desirable features. The very notion of a virtue presup- poses a set of ideals, a sense of what people in a particular society are supposed to strive for and admire. The virtues may be very rare in practice, as some Christian saints have exemplified, or they may be fairly common, as Aristotle considered the Athenian virtues to be among the aristocracy. But virtues represent the ideals of a particular ethos, its conception of its own ultimate purpose, or *telos*. Aristotle saw his society primarily in political terms, as an enlightened but embattled aristocracy trying to survive, whose members were trying to get on well with one another. A medieval monastery recognized its telos in God, and its virtues were therefore piety and faith. Most Americans see this as a society that maximizes happiness through hard work, efficiency, and good use of leisure time. Our virtues, accord- ingly, tend to be psychological and economic, hard work and the other virtues of "the work ethic," a keen sense of play and a high premium on entertainment value. Virtues are, in general, useful to the society of which they are an essential part, but it would be a mistake to think that this is all that they are. To say that virtues originate in their usefulness or functionality is not to say that they are in fact useful or functional. A virtue may long outlive its usefulness and yet continue to play an essential role in the life of a community. What was once fully functional may now serve as an important ritual that helps to hold the society together and gives its members shared meaning and focus. What is most useful and necessary to the life of a community, on the other hand, may not be considered as virtue. Aristotle's Athens had an agrarian economy, for example, but the virtues of farming were never mentioned by him and remained clearly undeserving of his ethical attention. Until very recently, many Americans assumed that their natural environment was an unlimited resource that could be used as needed and abused without worry, and what we now recognize as essential ecological virtues were either unrecognized or ridiculed as an odd eccentricity of certain nature lovers. Now, with environmental disaster on our doorstep, we are of necessity developing or adopting new practices, new attitudes, and new virtues to go with them. Necessity is not only the mother of invention. It may also be the mother of virtue.

In our pluralistic society, it would be highly implausible to believe that there is a single set of virtues and vices for everyone, even if it is equally absurd to suggest, as many self-help psychology books do, that each of us has our own unique virtues that are ours alone. (Nietzsche suggests this, in one of his more individualistic moods, in his long prose-poem, *Thus Spoke Zarathustra*.) There are some very general virtues that have to do with just basically getting along, especially the virtue of tolerance, but even this is not shared by all groups and it remains extensively qualified by many—for example, in those debates in which one or another moral principle is at stake, notoriously, the abortion debate. But for the most part, we will understand the virtues and the vices if we focus on particular communities and practices. In any community or practice, there will be more or less well-defined contexts or traditions in which certain clusters of virtues and vices become evident. These will, to a considerable extent, be functional and help the group to hold together and survive, sometimes by keeping out those who would subvert the purposes of the practice and split the community.

Taking as an example a community with a long tradition in which you are now embedded, let us take a look at the college or university community and its scholarly virtues. These are essential to studying and research, but they are also highly functional in reinforcing certain group standards and keeping out or eliminating those who do not follow them.

Some scholarly virtues:

- Being attentive, being thorough, paying attention to details
- Being trained, competent in the subject
- Being thoughtful and organized
- Having something to say that is new and interesting

- Being clear, and providing adequate argument and evidence
- Being serious (no fooling around)
- Being honest, quoting accurately, giving credit where it is due

We can readily understand why these should be virtues in the scholarly community—which includes the students, of course. We can also understand how these virtues would not be appropriate in another context, for example, in amateur sports or in an organization whose primary purpose was to provide fun and games for its members. Of course, the contemporary college or university embraces all three of these contexts—scholarship, sports, and social clubs—and there is or can be considerable friction between them, as every college or university president knows all too well. But in terms of scholarship and its application to teaching, the role and function of the virtues is amply clear. The overriding telos is *learning*. This does not, presumably, preclude having fun, but entertainment and enjoyment are to be encouraged only to the extent that they aid learning. Nor does this telos eliminate competition but, again, competition for grades and at the professorial level for grants and research results is to be encouraged or tolerated only to the extent that this competition furthers learning. What learning requires is, first and foremost, attention and attentiveness. Accordingly, the first virtue of scholarship is going to be paying attention. But a blank stare isn't going to count as a virtue. It is necessary to pay attention to details, to be thorough. A student should read other books on the subject. A scholar should read as many books on the subject as possible. A researcher sifts through all the evidence, not just the evidence initially favorable to his or her conclusion. He or she does not neglect or ignore competing hypotheses or interpretations.

It is also essential to be or get trained in the subject. Naïvete may be charming in an introductory class, but it wears thin soon and it is not long before it is humiliating. Incompetence is a term often abused as a way of eliminating the competition and expressing mere disagreement, but clearly no field of research can proceed or stay intact if there are no standards, no measure of competence, and no way of distinguishing good sense and solid work from flim-flam and incompetence. Competence is an essential virtue, then, but we should note that it is also a minimal one. To call a student or colleague merely competent in a letter of recommendation is to kill with faint praise. If competence is the virtue then genius and mastery are the ideals, of which competence is a merely pathetic shadow.

109

Being thoughtful and organized is a pedestrian virtue, but nevertheless essential. Nothing gets done without having a thesis, planning ahead, and not just throwing together a lot of facts and figures that don't lead or add up to anything.

Having something to say that is new, surprising, or thought-provoking may not be a virtue in itself—it rather seems like an accomplishment—but originality and creativity, or at least being in a position to recognize originality and creativity when one sees them, surely count as scholarly virtues, though one's less and less in evidence in the cutthroat college competition today. Originality and creativity are often conflated with profundity and "deep" thinking, but what is often presented as deep is only unintelligible, or as Nietzsche said of the romantics of his time, "They muddy the waters in order that they look deep." Being clear and presenting your research so that it is easily understood is, in academia, an often-neglected virtue that is akin to congeniality. On the other hand, being merely obvious or superficial, however clear and easy to understand, is no virtue either.

Being serious is a virtue that is greatly overrated, but it is no doubt essential to think that what one is doing, no matter how precious or irrelevant, is important. Humor has its place in academia, perhaps, but it seems that its place never concerns the worth of the study itself. Being honest is another much-neglected virtue among students and researchers, who find that the competition for grades and grants is getting too keen.

Giving proper credit for sources and stating the facts as you find them, not making them up as you need them, would seem to be basic to learning, for if scholarship and original research have a contrary, that contrary is surely willful misunderstanding and fraud. Plagiarism, accordingly, is not just cheating, and it is not just the violation of a moral rule. It may be true, as Kant argues, that widespread cheating undermines the very institution it was meant to take advantage of, and it may be arguable, with appeal to the principle of utility, that cheating ultimately hurts everyone. But what is more evident and immediate is that the person who plagiarizes other people's words and pretends that they are his or her own and the person who merely pretends to learn instead of pursuing learning just isn't the sort of person who belongs in the university community.

A discussion of the virtues in general may readily tend to vagueness and the sense that almost anything can be a virtue somewhere, under some conditions, but when we look at particular communities and their practices this tendency is dispelled and, if anything, the virtues emerge with remarkable precision and strictness. There is always room for disagreement, of course, and there will always be those who challenge even the most prestigious and central virtues of any practice and suggest some alternative. But this alternative is typically one of the other virtues of the practice, and the argument is often one of emphasis. For example, maverick professors may employ unusual teaching techniques to stimulate original thinking in their students, sacrificing some of the traditional scholarly propriety and seriousness accordingly. But the ultimate telos, learning, which requires good teaching, remains the same. Certain virtues are demoted in favor of others, but all within the already established practice. It is the shape of the practice that is altered, but not its essential dimensions. One can similarly gain an understanding of the virtues by taking any other communities or practice—whether it is football, foreign diplomacy, or fraternity pledging and initiation—and outlining its essential virtues and vices. If the larger theory of virtue ethics seems overly open and formless, the local precision of virtue ethics can be remarkable.

Over and above particular communities and practices, however, many virtue ethics still hold out the hope that there must be a single set of virtues and vices that define good and bad people as such, apart from any particular community or tradition. At the extremes, perhaps a certain constellation of vices would exclude someone from virtually any community or society. We can all agree, presumably, that someone who is selfish, inconsiderate, hostile to everyone, disrespectful of all rules, and indifferent to considerations of fairness, honesty, truth, and taste will tend to be unwelcome and potentially destructive in any group or practice. But here again, I believe that it is important to resist the temptation to reach for an all-embracing theory, and not just for the now standard multicultural reasons that people in different societies are significantly different and should be respected as such. It is also important to realize that almost every practice allows for certain exceptions, not just the maverick who shifts the shape of the practice, but also for the eccentric who creates a certain internal disruption and disharmony. In academia and the art world, perhaps, the celebration of eccentricity may be excessive and not, in fact, true of those respective communities. But other communities and practices have eccentrics too, and though these eccentricities may be intolerable in a large number of people, they are nevertheless essential for some. One example is the "wise guy," the person who, while participating in a practice (and perhaps participating in it much more seriously than he or she seems to), also makes fun of it and disrupts it. Several wise guys would destroy any practice (even the practice of being a wise guy), but just one such person allows everyone else to relax a bit and get a perspective on this practice that might otherwise be lost. Indeed, what would an American high-school class be like without one? Another example is the eccentric genius who risks being ostracized and being made fun of for wanting to take a practice beyond its current limits. Again, no practice can consist wholly of eccentrics, even geniuses, although a few eccentrics or geniuses keep a practice alive and invigorating. To insist that the virtues consist of those characteristics that everyone should have in a practice or in a society with a plurality of practices is to miss the importance of the exceptions. But, at the same time, to insist that everyone be an exception and to celebrate only the eccentric virtues is an equal absurdity. The virtues are bound to our practices, and it is only within the mutual cooperation and acceptance of a practice that there can be virtues at all. On the other hand, the virtues are as varied as our practices, and it is the variety of characters and practices that we consider, as a society and as individuals, to be our greatest virtue.

HAPPINESS AND THE GOOD LIFE: SATISFACTION AND SELF-ESTEEM

The promise of virtue ethics was that it would bring together the demands of morality and the pursuit of happiness. We have, thus far, discussed the nature of the virtues and morals, but we have not yet explored the notion of happiness. Living the good life, on the one hand, surely means doing good, acting in the right way, having the virtues. But, on the other hand, the good life also means living well, getting some pleasure out of life, and enjoying oneself, being happy. But what is happiness? And how does happiness link up with the virtues?

According to Aristotle, the linkage is virtually by definition. Happiness is simply the name of the good life, and it subsumes the virtues as an essential part of its character. "Happiness is the life of activity in accordance with virtue," he tells us. But the word "happiness" can be misleading. It seems to be something quite concrete and specific, but it in fact it covers a great deal of territory. We often talk as if happiness were a particular feeling, but this, at least, is exactly what happiness is not. Feelings can last for only a few minutes, but happiness—as opposed to merely momentarily feeling happy—is the

overall measure of a good life. ("I thought I was happy, but then . . .")
Aristotle tells us that the word translated as happiness (*eudaimonia*) is
nothing more than the name of the ultimate good or *telos* in life, that
toward which all our activities and our hopes are aimed. It thus
remains to be seen what particular goals, activities, and achievements
constitute happiness.

Eudaimonia is often translated as *doing well* or *flourishing*, suggesting
that success and happiness, properly understood, are one and the same.
Of course, here success means something more than simply doing well
in one's career or earning a good deal of money. The good life,
Aristotle tells us, is defined in part by one's status and respect in the
community, the esteem in which one is held by his fellows, and this,
presumably, is what most of us mean by success. Thus it is worth noting that the Greek term for virtue (*arete*) can also be translated as
excellence. To be good at what one does and to be a good person are
thus intricately tied together, and Aristotle would have little patience
or understanding for people who wholly divorce their work from
their personal life. Furthermore, living well means living together, and
political participation in one's community is not to be considered
merely an obligation or an unpleasant necessity. It is part of living well.
Notice how Aristotle ties all of these concepts so closely together that
it becomes impossible to make our modern distinctions between self-
interest and altruism, the personal and the social, success and happiness. It is, perhaps, because we tend to separate these concepts that we
create so many moral crises and conflicts of interest. We distinguish
and separate morality and happiness and then overemphasize the
threat of temptation and the need for self-sacrifice. We separate success and virtue and then complain about the number of unscrupulous
professionals and we wonder how a person can keep his or her
integrity and be successful. Aristotle, by contrast, puts all of these in a
tight conceptual package. That is why it is important to insist that the
good life is being virtuous and happy and not just being moral. Virtue
is already part and parcel of happiness while the Kantian conception
of morality, at least, separates the two. Of course, being virtuous does
not guarantee happiness: one can always be struck by tragedy despite
one's virtues. But the two concepts, virtue and happiness, are not to
be opposed, and there can be no happiness without virtue.

Hedonists would say that the good life is the life of pleasure. Many
moralists, in response, would be horrified. But in a sense, Aristotle
would not disagree. One could not be happy without pleasure in life.
But that is why it is important to remember that the test of having a

113

virtue, according to Aristotle, is that one enjoys its exercise. To live the virtuous life is already to enjoy life, to be pleased with oneself and who one is. One does not have to force oneself to be virtuous, and one does not have to overcome temptation. However much the glutton enjoys the food, the virtuous person enjoys his or her modest amount of food and his or her virtue, and without the possibility of embarrassment or humiliation. To be virtuous is not self-sacrifice or giving up what one wants. To be virtuous is to want to be virtuous, and so the choice between doing what one wants to do and doing what one ought to do does not even arise. And because virtue is also excellence, the good life for Aristotle is an active life in which we are virtuous by doing our best in those activities through which we contribute to society and assure our own health and well-being. It is not a choice between virtue and success. In Aristotle's ethics, there is no room for the careerist whose ambitions eclipse his sense of virtue, just as there would be no room for a so-called moral person, who by leading a timid and minimal life, did nothing wrong only because he or she did virtually nothing.

Aristotle's own role as philosopher and his close association with the great statesmen of Athens meant that the virtues he listed were particularly appropriate for such men, and the accomplishments he was thinking of were largely in the public realm of politics and statesmanship. He rather took for granted the accomplishments of everyone else in society and virtually ignored the idea that they too could be happy. Of course, he acknowledged that they could have virtues, but they were only the virtues of some servile status—as a good servant, a good soldier, a good farmer, a good shoemaker—and, accordingly, they could be happy in, at best, some inferior sense. They could do their work and play their roles well and be content with their lives. But there is no justification for denying the possibility of happiness in the fullest sense to servants, soldiers, farmers, and shoemakers. Aristotle discussed the virtues and happiness of the aristocratic class as the virtues and good life of the excellent human being as such. But why should we accept this notion that the best life is necessarily the life of the wealthy and the privileged, the rulers? If we are to make use of Aristotle's notion of happiness, accordingly, it will be necessary to expand our vision and insist that happiness and the good life do not depend on having the good fortune to be born Athenian, free and healthy and well-to-do.

Aristotle has, understandably, often been called an elitist, and indeed, he wrote his ethics not for everyone, but for the elite. (The very word "aristocracy" means "rule by the best.") But Aristotle's insistence on the connections among happiness, virtue, and excellence can apply just as well to those of more modest means. What is important is that one does whatever one does as well as possible and thus makes his or her contribution to the community. Nevertheless, to think that everyone can be happy and anyone can be virtuous is, perhaps, an unwarranted optimism. Both happiness and virtue have preconditions, and perhaps a good or at least decent upbringing is one of them. Nevertheless, we are continually moved by stories of people suffering under the most tragic handicaps—chronic disease, horrible poverty, terrifying social conditions—who nevertheless manage to make themselves both virtuous and happy. Nevertheless it may well be that the good life may be a relatively rare accomplishment. Even if we expand our vision and insist that there is much more to life than being an Athenian aristocrat, the truly happy life may be exemplary and exceptional.

The exemplary hero, for Aristotle, was Socrates, and it is worth noting, in this regard, that Socrates was no aristocrat, even if most of his students were. Socrates presented us with an example that is both exhilarating and disturbing. He lived a long, healthy, vigorous life. He enjoyed many pleasures. Indeed, he seemed to enjoy just about everything. Most of all, he loved the personal interaction involved in arguing about philosophy with the brightest young men of Athens. It was like a contest to him, and he was, no doubt, the best. In the end, he chose to die, not because he did not love life but, on the contrary, because he loved it so much. He died, he tells us, for the sake of his soul—which he believed to be eternal. He may have had years of pleasure ahead of him had he chosen to escape from prison, but his life would no longer have been meaningful. He would have betrayed what gave it its significance. Socrates's extreme example underscores what is true for all of us, that living well is not just living a pleasurable life. It is living a *full and meaningful* one. Socrates did not distinguish between his life as a whole, his happiness, and his virtues. To say that he died for the sake of his soul meant that his death was an essential and necessary part of his life. Accepting death to make an important philosophical point was as natural for him as winning an argument or falling asleep at the end of a long day.

Not everyone, of course, is a Socrates. It is by no means easy to take him as an example—as our example—and even if one does so it is difficult to say exactly what it is one should then do or how one should live in order to emulate him. He was, one might say, one of a kind, but this need not imply that none of us could possibly be virtuous or exemplary. Indeed, one of the more appealing features of an ethics of virtue may just be that we are all, if we want to press for details, one of a kind, in that the exact composition of virtues and excellences that make us exemplary are not all the same. Happiness and the good life, accordingly, need not be defined in the elitist terms of Aristotle's analysis, and the virtues need not be confined to the restricted realm of the elite. For some people, happiness and the good life are conceived in terms of security and raising a family, while others see life as the opportunity to create some great work of art. The question is whether one lives a fulfilling virtuous life in pursuit of those goals. Some people seek power and prestige. There may be nothing wrong with this, but one needs to have a clear conception of why such goals are so important and how they can be virtuously pursued. Power, in particular, is a means, and it always invites the question, "The means to accomplish what?" Some people seek knowledge or adventure, and many people just want to be liked and respected by their friends. Some seem to be satisfied just being entertained, but even here, one might suggest that there are virtues and vices—taste, to begin with, and sociability as well.

Every life has within it its own possibilities for happiness, its own virtues, depending on the practice and the community in which it participates. The advantage of the analysis of virtue we provided in the preceding section—as opposed to Aristotle's analysis, which he misleadingly describes in generic terms as the portrait of an excellent human being—is that there is no need to evaluate or measure our lives in terms of someone else's standards or in terms so all-embracing that we need to feel left out, unhappy, or unvirtuous. We all participate in various practices, and we practice various professions and careers. Doing well or flourishing means succeeding in those practices in accordance with the virtues of the practice and enjoying it, as well. We aim at excellence and virtue not because we have to, but because we want to, because that is what defines who we are and who we want to be. This is not to say that anything can be a virtue, given the appropriate context, nor is it to say that skills and talents that are merely professional and not at all personal count as virtues. Being a good parent is a virtue; being a good accountant is not. Being kind and generous are virtues; being clever and skillful at sifting through evidence is not. There is considerable overlap between the professional and the personal, of course, but the point here is not to limit the virtues to the personal so much as it is to contain the purely professional. It is, perhaps, one of the ethical maladies of our times that we overemphasize and isolate our careers and too readily eclipse or at least cut them off from the more personal parts of our lives. Aristotle is certainly right, for us as well for his own time, when he insists that happiness and the good life essentially involve love, family, and friendship, as well as what we broadly call success.

One of the problems that Aristotle pondered, but perhaps did not solve, is what we would call the problem of priorities. Aristotle, like many philosophers following him, suggested that the goal for all of us is happiness, but he is quite clear that this does not in itself dictate any particular way to live and includes a great many ingredients in various proportions. Aristotle was at least a bit ambivalent about what he thought those proper proportions to be and what was, accordingly, the best way to live. In some of his writings, he suggests that the best life is the life of contemplation, which suggests a relatively solitary and inactive life of study, thought, and reflection. But elsewhere he argues that the best life is a full, active, social life, in which thought and reflection play some role but by no means dominate our time or our attention. There is a rather vigorous dispute today about what Aristotle means by the life of contemplation and by what he calls the intellectual virtues, although we can be sure that he does not recommend being a hermit. This tension in Aristotle's ethics between philosophical thought and public life suggests a danger that threatens all of us. It is usually easy enough to pick one ingredient of the good life that seems to us more important than any of the others—artistic achievement or success or athletic accomplishment, for example. But then it is not always evident how we are to fit in all of the other parts of the good life, especially those quiet moments of contemplation or relaxation or quality time with friends and family that may be the first to go in a busy life. For Aristotle, the problem was how to be a full-time philosopher and at the same time be a complete human being. For many of us, the problem is how to be dedicated and successful in school or career, good to our families and, simultaneously, be satisfied and fulfilled in our lives as a whole. The question, "What is the good life and how should I live?" is very much an open question, and it is by no means clear that any single set of virtues, ambitions, or accomplishments provides a ready answer for everyone.

This problem of priorities—how to give proper weight to competing demands on our attention and our talents—seems to have increased in the past century or so. The German playwright and philosopher Friedrich Schiller complained about the "fragmentation" of life at the turn of the nineteenth century, followed by Karl Marx who fantasized about the time when "man could once again be a fisherman in the morning, a hunter in the afternoon," and no longer be restricted by the narrow specialization of modern life. We would like to think of what Aristotle called "the good life for man" as a single universal goal, common to ancient Greeks, medieval Chinese, and modern Americans, but we are aware of cultural differences—and the legitimacy of these differences—in a way that Aristotle refused to recognize. One central characteristic of our own circumstances is the specialization of our lives, the fact that most of us are expected to do one sort of thing and spend at least half our adult waking lives doing it. Specialization is more with us than ever before, and with it comes the vital set of choices faced by every college student: "I can't do everything, so what things should I do?" Ours may seem to be a life richer than almost any ever known before, but it is also a life of roads considered but not taken, doors slammed shut, and ordinary experiences unknown and untried. This makes ethics an exceptionally important enterprise, for there is a sense in which what we are choosing when we choose a career—whether medicine or business, entertainment or law—is an ethos, a way of life, with a set of goals and values that go with it. Whether or not there are any right answers for such personal choices, there is, nevertheless, the need to know the alternatives and the exigency of making the choice that best suits our temperaments and our talents.

Even if we agree that happiness is a life of activity in accordance of virtue, many questions still remain unanswered. For example, what is the role of desire and satisfaction in the good life? Happiness is often thought of as the satisfaction of all (or at least most of) our desires. Of course, it would be absurd to say that a person is flourishing if virtually all his or her desires were frustrated and all of his or her ambitions ended in failure. But there are at least three reasons to qualify the apparently plausible view that happiness as flourishing is the satisfaction of our desires. The first is intended to blunt the overly egoist interpretation of satisfaction, that satisfying our desires is essentially a matter of self-interest. The fact is that many of our desires and much of our happiness are, in an important sense, not just "ours" at all. For example, someone's life and happiness may be bound up in the well-being of one's family, or the success of one's business firm, or the thriving of the community. These goals may still be the object of one's desires, but it would be misleading to suggest that happiness is just the satisfaction of one's own desires; it may be the satisfaction of other people's desires and other standards and goals, as well.

Indeed, this fact led Aristotle to make the odd suggestion that a person's happiness continues after he or she is dead, for the goals and standards desired in life—for example, the success and happiness of one's children—continue after one's life is over. Of course, this concept would make no sense at all if one were to think of happiness as a feeling.

The second reason for hesitating to accept the view that happiness is the satisfaction of desires is the insatiability of some of the most important desires in life. They are never satisfied. Artists and writers are rarely satisfied once and for all. Each work is a step to the next. Thus, one sees the tragedy of young artists and writers who do their best work when they are very young, and spend the rest of their lives in that most unhappy state of "going downhill." Very religious people often insist that faith is more quest than conquest. Perfect faith, while an ideal to be striven for all one's life, is never actually attainable. Even pleasure may be important not so much in its enjoyment as in its pursuit. The great German poet Goethe has his lecherous character Faust exclaim, "From desire I rush to satisfaction, but from satisfaction I leap to desire." Happiness, in other words, need not be the product of our efforts, but may be those efforts themselves. Or, as a French wit once put it, "Love desires not satisfaction but prolongation." So, too, it may be with life and happiness—not satisfaction but lifelong effort and continuing passion are what count.

The third reason for not thinking of happiness as the satisfaction of our desires depends upon the all-important difference between the satisfaction of our desires and the satisfaction of our selves, even if it goes without saying that self-satisfaction includes the satisfaction of a good many goals and ambitions, as well. It is this overall self-satisfaction, which incorporates within it our concern for the well-being of others and the ethos of our community, that is the ultimate meaning of *integrity*—a whole life rather than conflicting fragments of merely satisfied personal desires. For example, when it came down to the hardest decision of all, Socrates decided to forfeit his life in return for something much more abstract and intangible. He claimed that he accepted an unjust death "for the sake of his soul." In less religious language, we might say that he died for the sake of his integrity, his wholeness as a person, his sense of who he was. He satisfied himself in doing what he believed to be right, in exemplifying his virtue and satisfying the demands of a higher calling.

Philosophers and psychologists are forever finding new motives behind everything that we do—pleasure, power, sex, selfishness—but much of what we do is motivated by our concern with the self, an effort to feel better about ourselves and our place among our peers. How we feel about ourselves is called *self-esteem*. How we feel about ourselves vis-a-vis our peers is *self-respect*. The connection between them is intimate and obvious, but the difference between them is significant. Both of them are essential ingredients in happiness and the good life. Both of them are tied to the virtues.

Self-esteem is thinking well of oneself, liking oneself. This need not be essentially reflective, an explicit recognition of one's status in the world. It often seems to be how one feels about himself or herself, manifesting itself in the confidence with which one acts and talks and relates to other people. Self-esteem is self-conscious, of course—it is, after all, *self*-esteem, but self-consciousness is not the same as that rather sophisticated philosophical act called reflection. Self-consciousness can be the very ordinary experience of suddenly "catching oneself in the act" or being caught in the shower or in some awkward position by an acquaintance. One can readily be wrong about whether he or she has high or low self-esteem and, as other people will be quick to detect, people with unacknowledged low self-esteem often act inconsiderate and arrogant by way of compensation. One may tie one's self-esteem to certain criteria of achievement or merit, but there are people who have accomplished a great deal and lack self-esteem, and people who have accomplished very little sometimes seem full of it.

Self-respect is a matter of one's place in a community. It is a matter of social standing and not so much a matter of what other people think of us or what we think other people think of us so much as it a reflection of what other people *ought* to think of us. Thus the glutton is typically said to have no self-respect, not because of what other people think of him but because he thinks so ill of himself. We recognize lack of self-respect in a person who goes to an important meeting unshaven or slovenly dressed, or gives a lecture unprepared, or talks about his sexual problems in a public forum. A physician or a professor loses his self-respect when he falls behind in his field. The public and the personal are not entirely separate spheres of life, of course, and so self-esteem and self-respect intermingle and overlap all the time. Accomplishment alone is not enough to guarantee either of them. In fact, a firm place in a warm community is usually enough to maintain both self-respect and self-esteem. In the absence of such a community, a lifetime of achievement may not suffice.

THE VIRTUES AND THE EMOTIONS:
CARING, COMPASSION, LOVE, AND FRIENDSHIP

Aristotle defends the essential role of reason in happiness and the good life, but he gives equal attention to the importance of having the right perceptions, emotions, impulses, and desires. Many of these feelings have to do with friendship and fellow-feeling, the bonds that hold us together not because of prudence or obligation, nor even as a means to happiness, but just because we are social animals. We care for one another. We live in families and communities not because we have to, but because we want to. "No one would choose to live without friends," insists Aristotle in his *Ethics,* and it is worth noting that nearly a fifth of that book is devoted to the nature of friendship as an essential part of the good life. So, too, Plato devoted two of his best-known dialogues wholly to the subject of *eros,* or love. The virtues of affection and fellow-feeling were essential virtues for the Greeks. To be happy and virtuous, one needed to care about people and be cared about in return. One needed friends and a family, love and affection. To be sure, the continuing warrior-mentality of the Greek philosophers did not allow them to express sentimentality about such subjects, but there can be no doubt that such feelings constituted an important part of Greek life, Greek ethics, and the Greek concept of the admirable person.

By contrast, what has struck many critics about modern ethics is the neglect and even contempt displayed for such personal emotions. Of course, it can be argued that deontologists such as Kant do not disdain the passions; they just dismiss them from the realm of practical reason. Kant had many friends, and according to personal accounts was a warm and friendly person. But in an infamous passage on loving thy neighbor, Kant remarks that such love must be commanded by reason as a duty and cannot be the "pathological" love of "melting compassion." The sarcasm is obvious (although "pathological" in this context means mainly "of the passions" rather than diseased), and the general tendency of modern ethics has been to consider the emotions, where they are not seen as a threat to rational thinking and dispassionate judgment, as pleasant or painful experiences to be calculated into the utilitarian accounting procedure. And while most of modern ethics puts a great deal of emphasis on personal morality and the public

121

interest, relatively few authors spend much time talking about the more limited relationships that exist between two or just a few people, in friendship, in the family, in love.

One of the aims of virtue ethics, accordingly, is to reintroduce an appreciation of the emotions and intimate personal relationships as part and parcel of our consideration of character into the core of our ethics. This is not a novel enterprise, even in modern times. In the eighteenth century, a group of virtue ethicists including David Hume and his friend Adam Smith (who also wrote *Wealth of Nations*, the bible of capitalism) defended an ethics *of the moral sentiments,* in which such feelings as sympathy and compassion provided the foundation for all of ethics. Jean-Jacques Rousseau, another friend of Hume's, defended a theory of the natural sentiments as well. But perhaps the most powerful impetus behind this movement today comes from a number of feminist authors, who have insisted that the history of ethics has been dominated by male authors who have presented a distinctively male ethic of rational principles as if it were the whole of ethics. In an important book entitled *A Different Voice* in 1982, Carol Gilligan, a professor of educational psychology at Harvard, suggested that women tend to think about ethics primarily in terms of personal attachments and relationships, not in terms of abstract principles of obligation, as men do. She was specifically attacking a colleague of hers at Harvard, the psychologist Lawrence Kohlberg, who had long suggested that a Kantian-type deontological conception of ethics was the only fully mature conception. According to this criterion, young boys reached ethical maturity at a rather young age, while young girls seemed to get stuck at an earlier, less mature stage of moral development. Gilligan, in reply, argued that the paths of moral development were different, and the very nature of fully developed ethical values was quite different in men and women. The argument concerning moral development, however, presupposed an important philosophical claim, namely that there were at least two different kinds of ethics. Some feminists, consequently, began to argue the superiority of the feminine ethic of caring. For example, Nell Noddings argues, in a book entitled *Caring*:

> One of the saddest features of this picture of violence [in the world today] is that the deeds are so often done in the name of principle. . . . This approach through law and principle is not, I suggest, the approach of the mother. It is the approach of the detached one, of the other. The view to be expressed here is a

feminine view. . . . It is feminine in the deep classical sense—
rooted in receptivity, relatedness, and responsiveness."

Feminist ethics, accordingly, has become one of the most important influences in ethics today. It finds a natural ally in virtue ethics,
although, to be sure, there are as many different versions of feminist
ethics as there are of virtue ethics, and only some of them display genuine congruity and agreement. But in the broader sense, and without
delving into the question of feminist politics, we can appreciate the
importance of the moral sentiments and the passions of close and intimate relationships for happiness and the good life. And for those who
do not take dispassionate reason as itself the highest virtue—what
some psychoanalysts would call dissociation—we can also appreciate
the demand that an admirable person will also be a passionate person
who is concerned about other people and cares deeply about his or
her family and loved ones. Hume, Rousseau, and Aristotle believed
that these personal attachments are of ultimate importance. Sympathy
for strangers and the broader moral outlook are possible only as pro-
jections or extensions of such personal concerns. What makes us
moral, first of all, is our personal concern for those closest to us.
Secondarily we learn to have similar concerns—even if based on principles rather than personal attachments—for the many people we have
never met and for humanity in general.

Hume, Smith, and Rousseau all describe the moral sentiments as
natural. They are unlearned and they exist in everyone, although they
can be destroyed by ill-breeding or, according to Rousseau, by the
"corruption" of competitive society. The sentiment of compassion,
literally *feeling with,* is the most basic of our social feelings, according
to these authors, the basis of all morality and the emotional glue that
holds society and, eventually, all humanity together. But the importance of compassion in ethics goes beyond its power to motivate
generous and helpful actions. It also indicates what is so suspicious
about the harsh dichotomy between morality and selfishness and the
arguments that play one off against the other. Compassion, as an emotion, clearly has the power to move us. Indeed, we often act out of
compassion without thinking about our behavior at all, leaping to
another's aid on impulse or feeling sorry for someone even before we
understand what is wrong. But the point of compassion is always
another being's interests and well-being, not one's own. One can, of
course, have compassion for animals as well as people, but it does not
make much sense to talk about having compassion for oneself, though

we do talk—disparagingly—of self-pity. But this means that at least some of our most spontaneous behavior is not in any way selfish. It is concerned with another person's well-being and therefore of an aspect of morality, not merely a personal impulse.

Compassion, according to Hume and Rousseau, is a sentiment that we feel toward any other person or creature, whether he or she or it is a member of our family, the family pet, a personal friend, or a complete stranger. We can feel compassion for any person or creature in pain. But some of the moral sentiments are not so open to anyone. They are very particular, sometimes even exclusive. A parent's love of her or his child or children is is such a sentiment. Such love might, in some rare instance, be generalized to include all children, but usually it is restricted to one's own children and very exclusive. Friendship is a variety of love. The Greeks called it *philia,* in contrast to *eros,* which is something like what we call romantic love. Friendship, too, is essential to ethics and the good life, and it is shocking how it has been left out of a great many moral theories or merely confined to the margins. When Aristotle insisted that no one would want to live without friends, he was not just projecting his own personal dependency. He was stating what he took to be a basic law of human nature, an indubitable presupposition of both virtue and happiness. Friendship, too, is exclusive or, at least, restrictive. It is possible for a person to feel friendly toward almost everybody, but, for most people, one's true friends are few in number, a small, select group of those whom one knows and cares about most. Love is even more specialized than friendship, often limited to members of one's own family or intimate group, and romantic love is an emotion often described by its limitation to one and only one person, as exemplified in the social institution of marriage. If love and friendship are virtues, therefore, they stand opposed to all of those conceptions of morality that insist on the centrality of general principles and universalizability. The moral principle "do not lie" applies equally to everyone and to every situation. The virtue of love may be restricted to a single individual.

There is a variety of love, sometimes called *agapē* or "Christian love," that is sometimes said to apply to everyone, everywhere, without discrimination. It is the emotion commanded in the New Testament by Saint Paul, and it is the love that is sometimes equated with God (as in John 4:16, "God is love"). It is, however, still love, an emotion with a concern for particular people, even if for everyone. Moreover, it is not just a spontaneous feeling, which one may or may not have. It is a commandment, an obligation. Thus we can sense the curious conceptual trouble that Kant feels when he worries about whether the command "love thy neighbor" (Matthew 22:39) should be considered a *moral* command, a "categorical imperative." If love is an emotion, he insists, then it cannot be commanded, for it is not rational and not a matter of will. So it must be, therefore, a matter of reason, not the emotion of love. In more ordinary terms, what bothers Kant is the idea that we can *love* everyone. We can have respect for everyone, but love—passionate love—is quite another matter.

The idea that ethics and morality should be based on love, and that love is the basis of the good life, has of course been the center of much of our thinking for centuries. It is central to the ethics of the New Testament, and it is central to not only the religions of Judaism, Christianity, and Islam, but many eastern religions as well. Hundreds of years ago, the troubadours crooned the virtues of love in France, and only a few years ago, the British rock group, the Beatles, sold several million copies of a song called "All You Need Is Love." As a basis for morality, the view here is a slightly more elevated version of the Hume-Rousseau thesis that all morality is a projection of personal fellow-feeling, now as love instead of compassion. The ethics of love is often equated with Christianity, but it is clearly defensible without religion; indeed, many of its most prominent defenders in recent years have not been religious at all. But in any case, the ethics of love— whether in the Bible or in New Age philosophy—is an insistence that fellow-feeling is primary in ethics. Rules and principles should only come later, if necessary, when love has reached its limits.

Unfortunately, love and friendship do have their limits, and so too does compassion. It is almost impossible not to feel compassion for the sick child living next door or depicted close-up in a magazine or television photograph, but it becomes increasingly a stretch of the imagination to maintain such a personal reaction to sick children living on the other side of the country or the other side of the world and it is harder and harder to visualize suffering when it is not a few but thousands or millions who are afflicted. In a large society—even a relatively small Greek city-state of 25,000 citizens—fellow-feeling, love, and compassion have their limits as the bonds of caring and intimacy stretch thinner and thinner. When we are dealing with people we don't know and may not like, it is clear that we need some guide beyond our feelings. Thus Aristotle insisted that we need justice—a key virtue and an essential ingredient in morality—precisely when friendship and personal concern ends. Two thousand years later, Hume complained that our sense of sympathy became more and more diluted as those who were suffering were farther and farther away or in larger and larger numbers. Accordingly, he too argued for the importance of what he called an artificial, calculated virtue—justice. Justice, one could argue, is the natural extension of our care and concern for other people, from the realm of personal relationships and acquaintances to the larger realms of society, humanity and, perhaps, life itself.

THE VIRTUE OF COMMUNITY: JUSTICE AND THE SOCIAL CONTRACT

Not only individuals, but communities, too, have virtues. Foremost among these, perhaps, is the virtue of *justice*. A good community will also be safe, friendly, cooperative, and have many other virtues that make it both desirable to live in and desirable to live with, but justice has typically been singled out, from Plato and Aristotle to the recent work of Harvard philosopher John Rawls, as the crucial virtue of any community, institution, or society. Communities have often been described as extended families—and, indeed, in many societies they *are* extended families. Jean-Jacques Rousseau, in particular, suggested that the family is the initial model for any society. But as communities grow and expand they lose the sense of personal intimacy and interaction and such emotional attachments as compassion, friendship, and personal affection get stretched too thin. One might be expected to be generous and fair to one's friends and loved ones, just because that is an essential part of friendship and love. But one cannot be so directly connected or concerned with the hundreds of millions of people in his or her own country, much less with the several billion people in the world. And so our spontaneous feelings of community, compassion, love, and friendship have to be supplemented with a more abstract virtue, the virtue of justice.

Justice is usually said to have two primary forms: *retributive* justice and *distributive* justice. Retributive justice is essentially concerned with punishments, with assigning blame and punishing people in proportion to their misdeeds. Distributive justice is, rather, concerned with the distribution of the goods of society, in part as a matter of reward, but also in accordance with needs and a number of other factors. The two kinds of justice are often treated independently, but they share common structures and concepts, in particular the concept of fairness and the importance of the notion of *equality*. Retributive justice is based on the idea that everyone be treated fairly and as equal before the law. A poor man is not to be punished more harshly than a rich man, and two people who are imprisoned for exactly the same crime should receive similar sentences as well. In distributive justice, it is extremely important that a person be rewarded in accordance with what he or she deserves, and two people doing the same job equally well deserve the same salaries. To treat people unequally for irrelevant reasons—to punish a man or pay him less because he is black, for example—is a flagrant violation of justice. Fairness and equality thus become the central features of justice and the source of its most difficult problems. Justice as a virtue—whether of a person or of a community—has a great deal to do with how one treats people with regard to both fairness and equality.

FAIRNESS AS A VIRTUE

To have the virtue of justice is to judge and treat people fairly, not only because it is what one ought to do but because one wants to be fair. A just society is one that not only has the right rules and procedures in place but also *cares* about justice and gets greatly concerned about cases of injustice and unfairness. But what is just and fair, and how does one know? To begin with, we feel reasonably certain about many cases of *injustice:* the case of a father who receives the death sentence for stealing a loaf of bread for his starving children, the innocent student who is singled out for punishment as an example for the entire class, the enormous raise in salary given to the boss's incompetent nephew who hasn't shown up for work in a month. And in each example, we can begin to formulate reasons for thinking: here is a case of unfairness. The punishment should fit the crime and extenuating circumstances should be considered. Blame should be restricted to those who actually did something wrong. No matter how effective making an example of an innocent student may be in deterring others who may be planning to cheat, we feel that it is unfair to punish someone who is not, in fact, to blame. In the third case, we feel quite strongly that a person should get a reward only after earning it, and that being the boss's nephew is no entitlement to special treatment. Indeed, it may have been an injustice for him to get the job in the first place.

127

The notion of fairness does not provide much of a definition of justice, if only because we so often use the words fairness and justice interchangeably. But fairness, in general, points to an agreeable fit between rewards and punishments and right and wrong actions. To break the agreed-upon rules of a game is unfair; to break a promise is, among other things, unfair too. To punish an innocent person is unfair, but so is a punishment that is much more serious than the crime, for example, a life-term prison sentence for cheating on a college exam or going ten miles over the speed limit on an interstate highway. A punishment that is much less severe than the crime is also unjust (although the criminal will rarely complain). In the realm of distributive justice, the fact that anyone should starve or be homeless in a prosperous country strikes many people as a gross injustice, and for "the rich to get richer while the poor get poorer" is also a paradigm case of unfairness to a great many people who nevertheless may have no doubts about the desirability of "getting rich." But this means that merit alone cannot be a sufficient measure of justice.

TREATING PEOPLE EQUALLY
AS A VIRTUE

Theories of distributive justice, like theories of morality, tend to be influenced by politics and ideology, by religion, and by one's upbringing. Three theories are vigorously defended in the world today. The first insists on egalitarianism, on treating everyone as equals. On the most radical version of this view, it is unfair that anyone should have more than anyone else, and it is the role of the ruling body of the society—in most cases, the government—to redistribute the goods of society from the rich to the poor. This was the official view of the recently disintegrated world view called communism, although it was rarely practiced as preached even in the most fervently communist regimes. But a more moderate version of the egalitarian idea of distributive justice was defended by Karl Marx in the mid-nineteenth century and it continues to be the view of a large number of people around the world who would generally call themselves socialists. Socialism does not take the extreme view that no one should have more than anyone else. It is evident that some inequalities are essential if people are to have an effective incentive to work and if governments are not to become overly intrusive and oppressive. But the idea is that no one should have such great advantages that others are left with nothing. In advanced industrial societies, this has meant that there should be a "safety net" for those who are the least advantaged in society. In newly capitalist China, by contrast, the new slogan is "Some must get rich first." So egalitarian doesn't mean that everyone has the same, but rather that we should be concerned that everyone has at least enough.

But even at the level of the safety net, if equality does not mean that everyone gets the same, then the meaning of equality is by no means so obvious. A young child in need of care and education or an elderly person in need of constant medical attention may need much more in the way of material resources than a healthy, self-sufficient adult. Nor should the young child and the elderly person be treated the same. They need different kinds of help, and the costs may be wildly different. Thus Marx famously said, "From each according to [his] abilities; to each according to [his] needs." The idea is not to ignore all of the important differences between people, their abilities, and their needs. Egalitarianism, the virtue of treating people equally, requires the very opposite, paying attention to their particular circumstances and treating them accordingly.

Could radical egalitarianism be put into practice in any society as we know it now? Could a society cultivate a citizenry that would be willing to do their best without the promise or possibility of special reward? Could we get people to take risks and develop special skills without added incentives? Or would the attempt to form such a state inevitably degenerate into the political oppression and inefficiency of some of the more tragic twentieth-century regimes? But in defense of the socialist theory of justice, the theory need not insist on extreme formulations such that no inequalities, no personal ambitions, and no special rewards are allowed. It need only insist poverty and deprivation in a land of plenty are intolerable and it is the obligation of the wealthy, "the haves," to eliminate that poverty and deprivation among the "have-nots." The governing idea is that equality is the norm, and deviations from the norm must have some special justification. Excessive deviations, great wealth or poverty, are unjust and should be corrected.

Rights Triumphant: Libertarianism

In direct contrast to such views, the libertarian view of justice rejects the idea of the redistribution of wealth and is willing to accept even gross inequalities as unavoidable. In this view, governments cannot step in and take away one person's goods in order to benefit another without violating that person's *rights*. It does not matter how needy the second person may be and it does not matter how great the gap may be between the wealth of one and the poverty of the other. What is central to the libertarian theory of justice is the insistence that certain rights are inviolable, in particular the right to own and hold onto one's property. But the theory also insists that such ownership must be *legitimate,* and so it permits the government to take away ill-gotten gains and give them back to their rightful owner. Indeed, such government power is itself legitimate and necessary just insofar as it protects property rights. The question of legitimate ownership, however, can become something of a muddle. If one's family home was stolen seven generations ago from the original natives of the region, does one have legitimate ownership? And if most of the civilized land on the earth was taken by force and perhaps more than once from its original inhabitants, can the notion of legitimate ownership even be made intelligible? Nevertheless, on a smaller scale of consideration—e.g., the questions of taxation and welfare, which are forms of government redistribution of wealth—the libertarian stance is quite clear. The government has no right to take from some citizens to give to others. The libertarian need not be devoid of compassion for the poor and, indeed, one of the corollaries of some libertarian theories is that those who are well-off have an obligation—whether through Christian charity or *noblesse oblige*—to help those much worse off than themselves. What the libertarian objects to is being forced to do so.

A Liberal Theory of Justice

As socialists become more tolerant of differences in wealth based on individual initiative and talent and the libertarian becomes more concerned with the condition of the disadvantaged in society, we start to see the way for a middle ground, a theory which takes seriously both the importance of equality and the notion of rights. The best known such middle or *liberal* theory today is the theory of justice developed by John Rawls in his book *A Theory of Justice* in 1971. Rawls defends two basic principles (quoted from the text):

1. The equality principle: "Each person engaged in an institution or affected by it has an equal right to the most extensive liberty compatible with a like liberty for all."
2. The difference principle: "Inequalities as defined by the institutional structure or fostered by it are arbitrary unless it is reasonable to

expect that they will work out to everyone's advantage and provided that the positions and offices to which they attach or from
which they may be gained are open to all."

In Rawls's view, inequities are inevitable in society, but there is a
rational way of justifying them. An inequality must benefit everyone,
not only the person who has a special advantage but, especially, people
who are the least advantaged. Thus it can be argued that it is fair to
allow some people to make fortunes from investments because, even if
their doing so makes them much wealthier than everyone else, it also
supports industry and improves the quality of life for everyone. But
Rawls is no utilitarian. Indeed, we saw in Chapter 2 that the utilitarian has a difficult time defending the theory against the accusation
that it provides no grounds for considerations of justice, for confronting an act that maximizes utility but only at the expense of violating the rights of some individual or small group of individuals.
Furthermore, utility may be maximized in the face of extreme
inequality and injustice, for example, if some undeserving people
become very, very rich and others, who may be much more deserv-
ing, do not suffer any particular harm. So Rawls rejects utilitarianism
and follows Kant as a deontologist. He develops his principles on
strictly rational grounds. He does not make a plea for compassion or
an appeal to personal self-interest. Like Kant, Rawls makes his appeal
to any rational agent, on grounds of reason alone.

The Social Contract

In defending his theory of justice, Rawls invokes a general conception
of justice that is in fact shared by a great many ethicists and most
Americans. It is the idea, derived in part from Kant's notion of autonomy, that people have the right to make agreements with one another,
and these agreements are then binding. The simplest example is the
making of a promise, making a commitment that you will pay back a
loan or show up for a recital or a party or keep a secret. A more formal
example of such an agreement is a contract, in which you explicitly
commit yourself to certain actions in the future, presumably in return
for some reciprocal action on the part of the other parties to the contract. Such agreements and contracts have a special place in our view
of ethics. It is one thing to be forced or fooled or cajoled into performing a certain action or behaving in a certain way, for example, the
way a young and somewhat mischievous child might be cowed or
tricked into behaving well for a new babysitter. But such manipulation

smacks of what we call *paternalism*, and while such imposition and control may be excusable and necessary for parents with young children, it is generally considered to be demeaning and inappropriate for adults. Adults like to think that they do what they do because they themselves chose to do it, and in much of morality and social life they like to think that they behave in a proper and ethical way not just because they were raised to do so but also because they, as well as everyone else, has agreed to do so. It is as if, according to this widespread and popular view, everyone in the society had signed a contract and formed an agreement. "I will not cheat or threaten you if you do not cheat and threaten me," and so on. Of course, there need not have ever been any such formal agreement or written contract—although our own Constitution is an exceptional example of such a contract. It is more as if it is implied in everything that we do. It is often called the *social contract*. And it is, according to many ethicists, the key to our concept of justice and fairness.

In the seventeenth century, the English philosopher Thomas Hobbes proposed such a model of human society. Hobbes was a radical thinker who, like so many philosophers, got in serious trouble for his ideas. In particular, he challenged the age-old and obviously self-serving doctrine of the divine right of kings. For Hobbes, the king ruled by agreement with his people, because he was necessary to hold society together, not because he was anointed by God. Hobbes suggested that, in *the state of nature*, before people joined together in society, they lived in a state of constant war of everyone against everyone. Life, he says, was "nasty, brutish, and short." And so people came together and agreed to a social contract, in which each person agreed to leave the others alone and give up certain rights to the king or sovereign.

Life became more peaceful and civilized, but the most valuable result of the social contract, according to Hobbes, was the concept of justice. There was no justice in the state of nature, only force and physical power. Now, in the web of agreements that tied men and women together in society, justice referred to their mutual obligations and expectations. Years later, John Locke developed a similar model of the social contract, which became one of the bases of the American Constitution, and Jean-Jacques Rousseau developed a continental version of the social contract in which he claimed that each person ultimately imposed the law on himself, rather than being forced by society to submit to its dictates. It is this idea of our imposing the law on ourselves, that is, choosing and agreeing to the rules by which we will live, that makes the social contract view of justice so appealing. Of course, none of these thinkers believe that there necessarily was such a contract. The social contract model rather establishes the idea of justice as mutual agreement. The principles of justice are not imposed on us by society. We have chosen them ourselves.

Rawls adopts the model of the social contract and asks us to imagine that we are in the odd but somewhat spectacular position of preparing to set up a society, in which we ourselves will have to live. In this situation the danger exists that we will each introduce self-interested suggestions. For example, if I am intelligent then I might suggest that intelligent people and jobs that require intelligence be richly rewarded. A man might well insist that men should have better jobs than women or get higher pay. A chronically ill person will probably insist that special care and attention be paid to the ill while a young, healthy person may make no provisions for the sick or the elderly at all. In order to neutralize such biases, Rawls suggests that we are subject to a "veil of ignorance," behind which we do not know what our position will be in society, whether we will be sick or healthy, intelligent or chronically retarded, male or female. We do not know whether we will be born into a family with wealth or a family in poverty, into a neighborhood that is safe and secure or a slum in which life is unsafe and insecure. And so we make our choices in a state of uncertainty. Since we do not know whether we will suffer some serious, debilitating illness or not, we would probably design a society such that people who do develop or are born with such illnesses are taken care of. Since we do not know whether we will be born very poor, we would likely arrange society so that no one will have to suffer extreme poverty. Thus we all must be rational at least in the sense that we cannot just pursue our own self-interests but must take into account the interests of everyone. Ultimately, the virtue of justice comes down to the virtue of rationality.

Given the uncertainty of our future position in such a planned society, some people might be willing to take their chances, hoping that with luck they will be born healthy and wealthy and at least intelligent enough to make their mark in the world. But most people, Rawls surmises, would rather play it safe, and so they will minimize risk by designing a society that is as equal as possible. Most rational planners will design a society in which everyone has the optimum opportunity whatever the circumstances of their birth and in which those who are most disadvantaged will benefit from the society too. For example, we might very well be willing to give some people more power than others so that they can form a government, on the grounds that everyone will benefit from an orderly society (almost everyone would suffer in a society where there was equality but universal chaos). And we would very likely be willing to give that government the power to redistribute wealth, just in case we find ourselves one of the very poor. But in the interests of prosperity, we would probably also agree to a system of rewards such that people will work as hard as possible, thus benefiting the entire society as well as themselves. They may become wealthier and more powerful than everyone else, but the benefits that they produce for the rest of society make this inequality more than tolerable. Thus equality remains the ideal, but it is offset by the recognition that inequalities may, within certain limits, be of considerable benefit to everyone. To be just is to see the world in this way and see more or less clearly one's place in the overall scheme of things.

EQUALITY, OPPORTUNITY, MERIT, AND ENTITLEMENT

We have not yet answered the question, what is equality? A belief in equality is not the claim that everyone is naturally endowed with the same abilities and talents. Some people are born with talent and intelligence, while others are not. Some people are reared in loving homes with good examples of happiness all around them. Others are raised in miserable circumstances. It is also not the claim that everyone can make equally valuable contributions to society. A student who works his or her way through the local urban night school with mediocre grades because of having to work all day may never be in a position to make the dramatic contributions to society possible for the well-bred Yale graduate who is born into political connections and power. We might hope that both of these students make contributions to the best of their abilities, but we would not thereby say that their contributions have equal impact or equal value. Equality of *results* seems to be an impossible aspiration, even in the most egalitarian society.

In the arena of education, at least in a democratic society, the issue of equality seems to turn on the idea of equality of opportunity. Is there any sense in giving two children the same educational opportunities when one, with proper training, will obviously learn a great deal, while the other, even with an exhausting effort, will learn very little? Of course, we could be wrong about their potential. A bright child may never fulfill his or her promise, and the slow student in the back of the class may emerge as a great scholar or scientist. We could say that all students deserve *equal opportunity,* but since even very young students enter school with very different abilities and backgrounds, this cannot simply mean that everyone should receive exactly the same education. The problem with treating everyone equally is that the best students will be unchallenged, while the poorest students may be left behind. We might insist that each student should be educated to maximize his or her potential for the good of both self and society. But if we do not have the resources for such an educational program, how should we make our choices? Some students begin with considerable educational advantages. Should *they* be given special consideration at the expense of everyone else? Some students begin with severe educational disadvantages. Should *they* be given special attention at the expense of everyone else? If the worst students cannot utilize the same opportunities as the best students, should the better students therefore be penalized? In his perverse short story, "Welcome to the Monkey House," Kurt Vonnegut suggests an intricate system of handicaps—to make strong people weaker, graceful people clumsy, beautiful people plain, and smart people distracted—all in the name of "equality." So, too, many recent political thinkers have objected that the emphasis on equality in modern society can have the disastrous consequence of encouraging mediocrity.

It has proven to be very difficult to formulate a notion of equality that is not hopelessly vague and that will do the important political work we want it to do. Nevertheless, some notion of equality is essential to justice, to ensure that people are given more or less equal opportunities for advancement and the good life and are punished similarly by the law for the crimes they commit. But equality is not the only factor in our notion of justice, even in our unusually egalitarian society. We also insist that people get what they *deserve*—punishment for their crimes, rewards for their contributions—and in this sense, we insist on treating people unequally. We summarize this aspect of justice with the word *merit.* People make different contributions and so deserve different rewards from society. We also insist that, even if people do not contribute as much to society as we would like, they should be rewarded (or punished) for *effort* (or lack of it). We also believe that people should be rewarded for setting an example, whether or not they personally produce anything as such, and that people in positions of responsibility deserve extraordinary reward, just by virtue of their visibility and responsibility. Sometimes, we are willing to reward people extravagantly just because they are popular and command a sizable share of the mass market for entertainment. We also believe that people should be rewarded, sometimes extravagantly, for taking risks (and not always very great risks), for example, when they invest money in a new product or real estate. Justice *entitles* people to certain goods, perhaps because they have worked and earned them, but perhaps even if they have not worked for or earned them in any way. If a dying parent gives everything away to his or her child or to an old college roommate, that is a private decision, and— no matter how undeserving—the child or the roommate is thereby entitled to the inheritance. Of course one might object to the advantages and abuses of inheritance, but our sense of justice currently includes some such sense of entitlement.

Finally, justice requires that those who cannot care for themselves be cared for, whether or not we want to defend the general Marxist conception of justice, to each according to his or her needs. It is not just compassion or charity that prompts us to change the plight of those who are without family and without means of support. There are levels of deprivation and inequality that no civilized society can or should be able to tolerate. In any considerations of distributive justice, that is the bottom line. No one should be left with nothing. If we have the virtue of justice we care about the well-being of other people, particularly those who are worst off.

VIRTUE VERSUS MORALITY: NIETZSCHE'S RADICAL VIEW

The virtues of justice and compassion discussed above have not been considered virtues by everyone, however. Insofar as our concept of justice or our feelings of compassion drain our resources and our energies away from our own excellence, there may be reason to object to it. While we have seen that virtue ethics is compatible with the modern moral philosophies of Kant and Mill and can expand and enhance traditional moral theory, some proponents of virtue ethics would emphasize the importance of personal excellence to such an extent that it eclipses considerations of morality and justice. One of the most radical advocates of virtue ethics is the German philosopher Friedrich Nietzsche. Nietzsche did not defend virtue ethics as a complement to morality. He used virtue ethics as a weapon to attack the very idea of morality. Nietzsche is often called a *nihilist* because of his uncompromising rejection of morality, but we should start with the insistence that Nietzsche was no nihilist. He did not reject ethics as such, nor did he (usually) insist that everyone has his or her own values. Indeed, his argument against morality was first of all that most people shared and were forced to share the same values, without regard to their individual talents, virtues, or differences. Furthermore, the values they shared were typically of a pathetic variety, notably, the pursuit of pleasure and security. Nietzsche therefore rejected the abstract, universal rules of the Kantians as well as what he considered the rather "vulgar" emphasis on pleasure and "utility" in the utilitarians. He focused instead, as Aristotle had long before him, on the exceptional character, the great-souled person who rose above the rest, *hoi poloi,* the "herd." Nietzsche praised the more than human hero who passionately pursued his or her own way, whether or not this accorded with that system of principles and prohibitions called morality. In fact, Nietzsche's attack on morality is not so much an attack on the substance of moral principles as it is an attack on the very idea of universal principles and the timid, herd-like motives that lie behind them. But behind his warrior Conan-the-Barbarian rhetoric, we might note, Nietzsche believed in keeping his promises and being a good neighbor. He did not believe in hurting people, and one of his last acts in life was to save a horse from a beating. What he believed, however, was that at least some people could be better than they are and that the idea of morality, rather than improving them, made them simply mediocre and ordinary, not admirable or exceptional at all.

The Kantian emphasis on intentions suggests that we know the motives that lie behind our actions. But what if the motives of even our most exemplary moral behavior were in fact selfish or self-interested, as the psychological egoist might argue? What if our most altruistic intentions were rather a devious strategy for winning the other's approval or gaining an advantage over him? Even Kant admits (a century before Freud) that we may not be conscious of all of the motives of our actions. He only insists that the moral worth of our actions must be measured according to those quite conscious intentions involved in acting on principle. His emphasis, understandably, is on those estimable intentions, such as "wanting to do one's duty" and "showing respect for the law." So, too, philosophers who would rather emphasize emotions and other inclinations that motivate our behavior—David Hume, for example—emphasize our more benign feelings, such as sympathy, love, and fellow-feeling. But suppose the springs of action were not so noble and the motives for morality were not so much concerned with duty, compassion, and fellow-feeling. Suppose even the most benign feelings were really a front for hostility, competitiveness, and timidity, just as biologists have suggested that the human smile originated as a sign of submission. Suppose the dominant motive for morality was not the desire to do one's duty, but rather fear or some other pathetic emotion. What would we say about morality then? And would we still feel, as we now do, that morality ought to have trump status among our various rules and principles?

This drastic challenge to morality has always been around. Socrates had to argue against it in the early books of Plato's *Republic;* Saint Augustine was painfully aware of its possibility. But the thinker who is most responsible for elevating this suspicion about morality to a full-blown philosophy is Nietzsche. Morality, he argued, is not motivated by duty or respect or love or sympathy. It is motivated by fear, envy, and resentment. Much of traditional morality, he pointed out, has been motivated by the hardly honorable emotion of sheer terror—of one's masters, of the king, and, most of all, of God. Millions may have walked "the straight and narrow" in order to avoid the everlasting flames of hell, but that scarcely entitles them to any claim to nobility. Action for the sake of duty may be honorable, even admirable, but action based only on fear is timidity, or at best prudence, not virtue.

It is not fear that Nietzsche cites as the most vicious motive of morality, however. Indeed, fear at least is straightforward and usually doesn't pretend to be more than it is. It is otherwise with those virulent motives of envy and resentment, both of which are vengeful emotions. Indeed, Nietzsche sometimes characterizes morality itself as "the greatest act of revenge in history." Revenge for whom? And against whom? Nietzsche tells us that it is the revenge of the weak against the strong, of the losers against the winners, of the slaves against their masters. Thus Nietzsche distinguishes between "master morality" and "slave morality." Master morality—or what Nietzsche elsewhere calls "noble morality"—is an ethics of virtue and excellence. It is concerned only with the best and most admirable people. Slave morality—what in contemporary parlance and Kant's philosophy is simply called morality—is a reactionary value system that rejects the virtues of the powerful and privileged and substitutes for them ordinary virtues: meekness in place of strength, humility in place of pride, innocence in place of experience, ignorance in place of wisdom, and so on. The commandments of morality, accordingly, are meant to discourage the virtues of the most exemplary members of society and to encourage the timid mediocrity of the untalented, the uncreative, the powerless.

Morality thus consists of prohibitions against the strong for the protection and edification of the weak. Why else, Nietzsche suggests, would so many of our moral principles be *negative*, "Thou shalt not . . . "? How else can one interpret such promises as "The meek shall inherit the earth" and "It is easier for a camel to pass through the eye of a needle than for a rich man to enter the Kingdom of Heaven"? These are the expressions of envy and resentment, the bitterness of those who do not have power, wealth, and earthly glory against those who do have them. Morality, Nietzsche concludes, is not the noble aspect of our lives that we have pretended. It is an expression of weakness and therefore ignoble and hypocritical, pretending to be something that it is not. Morality is a diabolically clever strategy invented by the weaker and more impoverished members of society to protect themselves from the stronger and more powerful. It restricts the ambitions and curbs the desires of those who would be superior and transgress the rules that enforce civil behavior and universal mutual respect. Universal principles are not a function of practical reason, but a form of leveling, keeping the best people down by pretending that everyone is really the same. Morality is thus the enemy of excellence. Not surprisingly, Nietzsche defends a "great man" theory of history, according to which a society moves forward only by a handful of exceptional individuals—artists and thinkers, as well as warriors and diplomats—and the well-being of the average citizen is of only secondary significance.

Nietzsche has inspired many readers with visions of greatness as well as entertained them with his extremely witty, biting irony and his stinging critique of the hypocrisy and vacuousness of other moral theories. But it is so easy to get caught up in his dashing brilliance and the rousing encouragement to escape from the herd, we should insert a note of caution. What would it mean to create one's own virtues, as Nietzsche urges, and how would one go about doing it? And what if one is not, after all, one of Nietzsche's exceptional heroes? Is it so bad to act out of fear, or even resentment, if one has good reason to be prudent or is rightly offended or oppressed by others? What's wrong with pursuing security and happiness, in the perfectly ordinary sense? Is it justifiable to put so much weight on individual character apart from any concern for the public good? Aristotle, who defended virtue ethics twenty-four centuries before Nietzsche, would have dismissed Nietzsche's argument. A virtue for him was an excellence that was publicly defined and expressed in public performances, not a personal creation and a merely private sense of accomplishment. There is much to admire and even more to ponder in Nietzsche's attack on morality and defense of exceptional character, but it is a radicalism that should be read with caution, strong medicine that should be measured by how much one can safely swallow.

SAINTS, HEROES, AND ROGUES

Nietzsche's point about the inadequacy of morality to encourage excellence is one that has bothered traditional moralists, including Kant and Mill, for some time. Much of what is discussed under the name of morality has to do with fulfilling obligations and maximizing general well-being, doing what one *ought* to do. But what one morally ought to do is limited, and much of morality consists of prohibitions, rather than positive recommendations or ideals for action. Furthermore, as we have already noted, one problem with a conception of morality that is limited to obeying the rules is that a perfectly good person might also be an utterly unexceptional person whose behavior benefits and inspires no one. When morality becomes no more than doing one's duty, it becomes a dreary and often tedious matter. A self-proclaimed "immoralist," Nietzsche thus suggests that morality is essentially a leveling device intended to lop off the peaks of human excellence as well as to encourage the herd to behave themselves and feel good (even self-righteous) about themselves. But extraordinary behavior—heroic and saintly deeds—tend to get ignored in such a conception and, indeed, moral theorists in the Kantian mold have been hard-pressed to give an adequate account of those who go far beyond their moral duties to display such extraordinary behavior. Thus a special term has been invented for such behavior, which is "beyond the call of duty": *supererogatory*. Thus those exemplary acts and people that are at the very heart of ancient ethics are downgraded into a curious and problematic set of exceptions.

We can better understand the nature of these inspiring examples in the terms of virtue ethics rather than the terms of morality and obedience to principles. One of the most inspiring facts in ethics is that there are people who go far beyond the rules, not breaking them, but far exceeding their demands. Thus the good man, for Aristotle, is not just one who obeys the rules; he also excels in what he does. This is not to say that he disobeys the rules and laws of Athenian society; he just does not often think of them because they are second nature. The good man is expected not only not to flee from battle. He is expected to fight to the best of his ability. He is not only expected not to lie (which is easy enough if you keep silent); he is also expected to be witty and clever and informative, if not as brilliant as Socrates. People have always had heroes, and emulating heroes is among the oldest lessons in ethics. In the media today, we are still inundated with examples of heroes, although their personal excellence and exceptional virtue is not always as clear as perhaps it should be. Such examples may be far more appealing and powerful than the abstractions of morality, and we may well want to agree with Nietzsche that an ethics of heroism is far more inspiring than the mundane world of morality.

This idea of going beyond morality, beyond the call of duty, is also evident in those special people whom we designate as *saints*. A saint is not just someone who is perfectly good in the sense of not sinning. It is possible that he or she has not had the opportunity. A saint is extraordinarily good, resisting temptations that we cannot imagine resisting and doing good deeds that are far beyond the demands of duty or charity. Similarly, a hero or heroine is a person who does not do just what is commanded, but much more—indeed, much more than anyone could have expected. One cannot command saintliness or heroism, and it is no one's duty to be a saint or a hero or heroine. Nevertheless, our ethics would be impoverished without such models of behavior to aspire us to be at our best. Refraining from a forbidden act because of fear of punishment or anticipation of guilt may still count as moral, but it is nothing like, and does not feel at all like, that sense of what Aristotle and Nietzsche call nobility that motivates our best actions. Acting from a sense of duty may be motivated and accompanied by a comforting sense of righteousness, but the saint and the hero typically do not even think of what they are doing in such terms. Indeed, it may be in part that naïveté, the absence of self-doubt and deliberation, that may make a person a saint or a hero.

Saints and heroes have the virtues appropriate to their cultures. These will not, obviously, all be the same. The Christian saints had different virtues from those of the Buddha, and Saint Francis had different virtues from those of Mohammed and his first followers. Achilles and Alexander the Great had very different virtues from those of Gandhi and Martin Luther King Jr., and Einstein had a different set of virtues from those of Giordano Bruno, who was burned at the stake in 1600 for his scientific speculations. The virtues of the saints and heroes are not just the ordinary virtues that make a "good person"—honesty, trustworthiness, a sense of humor—indeed, their virtues may be such as to eclipse some of those more ordinary and domesticated virtues

141

altogether, particularly in times of moral turmoil. A person who is extremely devout may lack a sense of humor. A hero might very well not be a nice person.

The occasional conflict between virtues and moral rules, between the virtues themselves and in particular between the more ordinary virtues and the extraordinary virtues of saints and heroes helps to explain an ethical phenomenon of the *rogue*. Many familiar heroes and heroines in contemporary American literature and culture are rogues. The rogue is often a stylish figure, played in movies by a charming or seductive star. Typically, the rogue breaks the law, or at least is at odds with the law, and committing outright crimes is not unusual. In American movies, such outlaw behavior may include the violation of several dozen traffic laws within a ten-minute chase scene. In literary criticism, such a character is often called the *antihero*, a term that expresses the ethical confusion about the fact that the person has the status, but not the morals, of a hero.

Why should such a character be mentioned in ethics at all, except perhaps as an unfortunate popular example of rampant immorality? First of all, like it or not, these are the heroes and heroines who now provide the moral examples for millions of American children and teenagers, and one would be dangerously mistaken in relegating such figures to the supposedly fictional world of mere entertainment. Second, such examples illustrate quite clearly the complexity of our actual morals and moral conceptions, which are not limited to universal rules and obedience but include an admiration for those who dare to be different, so long as they are admirable or exceptional in some appealing way. Third, they highlight the enormous range of the concepts of virtue and of character in ethics.

It would be misleading, however, to leave the example of the rogue in the hands of American moviemakers, as if the sole occupation of such characters were the perpetration of financially rewarding felonies. There is a history of far more honorable rogues, who have compensating virtues go beyond superficial charm and attractiveness and provide rewards for society for generations to come. These rogues include many of the great artists of past centuries who were famously difficult people and often selfish and immoral as well. Whether they had to be so to be great artists, or became so because they were great artists, are two much-discussed but dubious hypotheses that we need not explore here. Beethoven scandalized most of Viennese society with his lack of manners and untrustworthiness, and before him Mozart carried on in a most improper manner. The great French author Balzac motivated himself to write by plunging deeply in debt with high living, and some of the greatest poets who followed him, such as Rimbaud and Baudelaire, led famously immoral lives in Paris. Picasso's moral eccentricities have been much publicized in recent years, but his behavior is not very different from that of a great many famous artists, male and female, in the bohemian culture in which the arts have flourished for the past century or so. In the realm of the intellect, Freud and Jung have often been accused of inconsiderate, if not immoral, behavior toward their psychoanalytic colleagues. Even Martin Luther has often been portrayed as a man who was deeply neurotic, frequently inconsistent, if not hypocritical, and cruel to many of those closest to him. And yet, given the enormous contributions of these rogues to our culture, it seems beside the point to dwell on their personal failings.

My point here is not to defend immorality. The behavior of rogues is rarely immoral in any repulsive sense. Otherwise, they would quickly lose their status as heroes of any kind. It is to make the point once again that our ethics is a complex and flexible system of concerns, as complex and as flexible as our pluralistic ethos. Indeed, one reason that rogues are so important to us is that they often attack corrupt or unreasonable authority, stand up for "the little guy," and represent the oppressed minority against the dominant and unsympathetic majority. Thus, despite their occasional immorality or criminality, the rogue may represent to us some of the virtues most prized in our society—independence, humor, initiative, a kind of courage, and a deep concern for others—which go beyond mere rule-following. To think of the rogue as simply immoral, therefore, is to miss his or her ethical significance. And to focus on a single moral exemplar who is guided only by duty is to paint an emaciated picture of ethics and present a grossly inaccurate portrait of our ethos.

ABSOLUTE VALUES, RELATIVISM, AND PLURALISM: AMERICAN MORALITY TODAY

Once upon a time, some people like to imagine, morality was a simple matter and everyone agreed on what was right and what was wrong. In such an uncomplicated situation, the question of justification would have seemed unimportant and the very idea of ethical relativism would have struck most people as absurd. It is unlikely, however, that there has ever been such a time. Every society, no matter how seemingly homogeneous, has produced its critics, its deviants, its doubters, its troublemakers. Sometimes, such people have been simply ignored, or ridiculed, or isolated. Sometimes they have been persecuted, tortured, exiled, or killed. Throughout much of history, those who questioned the ethics of their own culture have been condemned to silence, or worse. But today the world is a small place, television and the Internet are everywhere, and cultures are colliding, throwing moralities and values, as well as national interests and religions, into conflict with one another. Our own society is, if not a melting pot, a mixed salad, in which dozens of cultures coexist, many of them in the same city, on the same block, in the same schools and churches. Mutual examination, criticism, and conflict have thus become as inevitable as mutual tolerance is necessary.

Given this diversity and contact, one is more likely than ever to be forced to question his or her own values, perceive and appreciate alternatives, and seek some justification for this way of doing things or that one, or embracing this value or that. Aristotle presented a picture of Athenian morality that was a unified, generally agreed-upon whole, with no need for justification and not even a bow to alternative moralities. This self-promoting image is misleading, however, as even a cursory glance at the history of his time and place shows. Aristotle's Greece was a cauldron of cultural conflicts, both within Greek society and between Greeks and the so-called barbarians around them. In our own culture, the meeting ground for most of the cultures of the world, we acknowledge differences but still try to grasp a unified whole, using the term pluralism as if it were a single ethic rather than a constant battle for ethnic survival, ethical recognition, and moral superiority.

In recognizing the plurality of mores and morals by which we live, theories of ethics, especially in the United States, of many people have tended toward the idea that values are a matter of personal preference and opinion. At the same time, however, they continue to think of their own values as correct and respond to disagreement or opposition with considerable hostility. Consider such public ethical issues as the right to life of unborn fetuses, the justifiability of war, the justice of taxation, and the redistribution of wealth. Very few citizens have no opinion on these matters, and these opinions are by no means loosely held. This sets up a dangerous state of affairs in which, on the one hand, we cease to take questions of value (and the policies that these suggest) very seriously, and on the other hand, we take them so seriously that they are beyond discussion and negotiation. Consequently, it is often lamented that the quality of our public discourse has become unacceptably impoverished. Political advertising on television has sunk to the level of vicious attacks by way of thirty-second sound bites. Talk shows that are supposed to involve spirited, but intelligent, debate have degenerated to mere shouting matches. And too many people avoid talking about values or politics with anyone but those they already agree with, as disagreement is considered offensive and uncomfortable, if not perilous. Thus our pluralism tends to Balkanization if not outright mutual hostility, and the essential discussions that are necessary both for mutual understanding and for joint decision making become impossible.

The philosophical tension here, between those who insist on absolute values and those who insist on tolerance to the point of non-confrontation, is the source of the problem. Thus the difference between various ethical theories is obviously not just a philosophical problem, a matter of academic dispute between competitive professors. It may not ultimately matter whether one is a Kantian, a utilitarian, a moral sentiment theorist, or a virtue ethicist, but all of these views take values and morals seriously, and it is in the discussion and debate between them that we get clearer both about the nature of ethical disagreement and what we really believe and value. And the fantasy of a time when morality was simple and everyone agreed on what was right and what was wrong only makes the situation worse, as if holding one's ground for absolute values (namely, those that one happens to hold) has both historical justification and a promising future. Thus Alasdair MacIntyre half-jokingly comments, "forward to the twelfth century," suggesting an impossible plea to return to a mythical past. But the situation in current-day America is too much like that, but with many different mythical pasts appealed to. Too many different sets of absolute values confront one another, and because they are absolute they are not up for discussion and do not allow disagreement. In such a complicated situation, the question of justification is unavoidable and the idea of ethical relativism is not at all absurd. But relativism isn't the conclusion of the discussion. It is the beginning, and it is where we learn to understand one another and find pathways to sensible policies, if not agreement on at least some basic issues.

Instead, when we attempt to overcome our own perspectives, we try too hard to be "above" any particular society and culture and so, in the name of universalism, find ourselves nowhere at all. Or, we insist on rationally justifying our moral principles and end up wondering on what grounds—if any—we could condemn even a Hitler or a Stalin. But to have ethics is not to have a rigid set of moral principles with an ironclad theory of justification for them. It is to share a way of life in which certain values, practices, and rules of morality (including tolerance) play an accepted, but flexible and always open-to-question, role. To question everything is to be left with nothing, but to refuse to question at all, or to insist on an ultimate justification, relegates morality to the realm of stubborn habits and condemns a multicultural society to endless bitter moral and political battles. But we will never find ourselves living well so long as we believe that we are hopelessly confused and swimming in a veritable sea of values without any hope of common agreement, or that our group is right and everyone else is wrong.

What we need, therefore, is a new ethics of pluralism, an ethics especially suited to contemporary America rather than the ancient Greek polis or the small towns of Kant's eighteenth-century Germany. The naïve and lazy relativist view that "values are just a matter of personal opinion" must be recognized as just as nonsensical and dangerous as the dogmatic view that one's own morals are absolutely correct and everyone else is wrong. We are not a society without values, much less a society in which every act is no better and no worse than any other. But we are a society with a multiplicity of values, in which it therefore becomes all the more urgent for each of us to clarify, understand and, within modest limits, justify our values and our views. The *ethé* of many traditional societies are already established and in process of coming apart, but the complex ethos that constitutes American society is still in the making. It is by studying and discussing that we can assist in its formation and in doing so come to understand what living well really means for us.

Recommended Reading

M any of the classic texts discussed in this book are included, with commentary, in Robert C. Solomon and Clancy W. Martin, *Morality and the Good Life*, 4th edition (San Francisco: McGraw-Hill Book Co., 2004). There are many books now, and a great many good encyclopedia articles, on Kant and Kantian ethics and on utilitarianism. Particularly recommended are *The Routledge Encyclopedia of Philosophy* (London: Routledge, 1998) and *The Blackwell Companion to Ethics* (Oxford: Blackwell, 1991). The classic contemporary critique of traditional moral philosophy is Alasdair MacIntyre, *After Virtue* (Notre Dame: University of Notre Dame Press, 1981). Two good collections on virtue ethics are Michael Slote and Roger Crisp, eds., *Virtue Ethics* (New York: Oxford, 1997) and Peter French, ed., *Ethical Theory: Virtue and Character* (Notre Dame: University of Notre Dame Press, 1988). Two contemporary books on the subject are Michael Slote, *From Morality to Virtue* (New York: Oxford, 1995) and Christine Swanton, *Virtue Ethics: A Pluralistic View* (New York: Oxford, 2003). A wide variety of contemporary issues is in L. Bowie, K. Higgins, and M. Michaels, *Thirteen Questions*

(Belmont, CA: Wadsworth, 1992). Two good short discussions of contemporary issues are Peter Singer, *Practical Ethics* (Cambridge: Cambridge University Press, 1979) and James Rachels, *The Elements of Moral Philosophy* (New York: Random House, 1986). The classic book on justice is John Rawls's *Theory of Justice* (Cambridge: Harvard University Press, 1971), but this will be very difficult for the beginning student. Helpful essays on Rawls can be found in Norman Daniels, *Reading Rawls* (New York: Basic Books, 1977). A more general collection on the problem of justice is Robert C. Solomon and Mark C. Murphy, *What Is Justice?* 2nd edition (New York: Oxford, 2003). An excellent contemporary treatment of relativism is Robert Kane, *Through the Moral Maze* (New York: Paragon, 1994).

Index

Dignity, 70
Disinterestedness, 12, 62, 81
Divine purpose, 55
Divine right, 132
Divine spark, 56
Dostoevsky, Fyodor, 55

E
Edinburgh, 100
Education, 105, 134, 135
Egalitarianism, 102, 128, 129, 134
Egoism
  and altruism, 19–22, 92
  defined, 20–21
  and enlightened egoism,
    57–59, 75–77
  ethical, 21–22, 137
  psychological, 21–22
Egyptians, 101
Einstein, 141
Elitist philosophy, 40, 114, 116
Emotion, 80, 104, 121–126,
  137, 138
Emotional contagion, 61
Emotivism, 80
Empathy, 60–61
Enlightenment, The, 63
Equality, 63, 86, 127, 129, 134–136
  as a principal, 130
  of results, 134
Eros, 121, 124
Eskimos, 83, 85
Ethé, 146
Ethical altruism, 22
Ethical egoism, 21–22
Ethical relativism. *See*
  Relativism: ethical
Ethics (Aristotle), 77
Ethics
  and acting for reasons, 30–33
  and change, choice, and
    pluralism, 4–7

defined, 3–4
and egoism and altruism,
  19–22
and ethos, 7–8, 146
feminist, 122, 123
and great philosophers,
  37–41
history of, 37, 82
introduction to, 1–41
and justification, 88
and morality, 9, 90
and motivation, 25
and pluralism, 143, 144
and relativism, 15, 18–19,
and rules and virtues, 33–36
and virtues, 99–101, 105, 116,
  118, 121, 123, 137, 138
Ethos, 7–8, 146
  and ethics, 18–19, 48
  and morality, 74, 88
  and pluralism, 143
  and virtue, 98, 107, 118–119
Eudaimonia, 54, 113
Euthyphro (Plato), 52–53, 77
Evil, 76
Excellence, 93, 113–116, 136,
  138, 139
Exchange, 70
Existentialism, 40

F
Fairness, 127–128, 132
Faith, 53, 78, 92, 104, 107, 119
Faust, 119
Fearlessness, 105
Feminism, 122
Fragmentation, 117–118
Francis, Saint, 141
Free choice, 79
Free market system, 102
Freedom, 40, 105
Freud, 137, 143